MOON PARIS WALKS

Step out of your hotel and head right for the nicest neighborhood in town. Find out where to get the best coffee in the city or where to drink locally brewed beer on tap. Local authors share with you only genuine highlights of the city they love. This way, you can skip the busy shopping streets and just stroll through the city at your own pace, taking in some famous attractions on your way to spots where locals go to shop, eat, or just hang out. Savor every second and make your city trip a truly feel-good experience.

PARIS-BOUND!

You're about to experience Paris—the city of wide avenues, world-famous monuments, and of course la vie Parisienne. Start the day with a cup of coffee and a croissant, which—just like the locals—you can have in a café standing at a counter. Shop in amazing stores, from those of top designers to small, vintage boutiques in one of the city's charming neighborhoods. Don't forget to take in some culture with a visit to a museum or a walk in one of the many parks and gardens. Plus, there is good food and good wine to be had in every neighborhood. We'll show you where.

ABOUT THIS BOOK

Experience the city on foot and at your own pace, so you can relax and immerse yourself in the local lifestyle without having to do a lot of preparation beforehand. Our walks take you past our favorite restaurants, cafés, museums, galleries, shops, and other notable attractions—places in our city we ourselves like to go to and that we really enjoy. So who knows, you might even run into us.

None of the places mentioned here have paid to appear in either the text or the photos, and all text has been written by an independent editorial staff.

CITY
PARIS

WORK & ACTIVITIES
**FASHION STYLIST
& BLOGGER**

As a lover of all things fashion, art, and joie de vivre, it wasn't a big surprise that Roosje traded the Netherlands for the City of Light. Walking around the beautiful streets of Paris, looking for a nice terrace for a cup of coffee or an apéro is her favorite thing to do. She knows the city so well that even her Parisian friends ask her for the best spots in town.

LOCAL
ROOSJE NIEMAN

PRACTICAL INFORMATION

The six walks in this book allow you to discover the funnest neighborhoods in the city on foot and at your own pace. The routes will take you past museums and notable attractions, but more importantly, they'll show you where to go for good food, drinks, shopping, entertainment, and an overall good time. Check out the map at the front of this book to see which areas of the city the walks will take you through.

Each walk is clearly indicated on a detailed map at the beginning of each chapter. The map also shows where each place mentioned is located. The color of the number lets you know what type of venue it is (see the key at the bottom of this page). A description of each place is then given later in the chapter.

Without taking into consideration extended stops at any one location, each walk will take a maximum of three hours. The approximate distance is indicated at the top of the page before the walk description.

PRICES
Next to the address and contact details of each location, we give an idea of what you can expect to spend there. Unless otherwise stated, for restaurants the amount given is the average price of a main course. For sights and attractions, we indicate the cost of a regular full-price ticket.

GOOD TO KNOW
Paris consists of the area between the two ring roads that encircle the city: the Boulevard Extérieur and the Périphérique. Everything outside these roads is

LEGEND

● >> SIGHTS & ATTRACTIONS   ● >> SHOPPING
● >> FOOD & DRINK   ● >> MORE TO EXPLORE
☼ >> WALK HIGHLIGHT

considered the banlieues (the outskirts). The River Seine runs through the city, splitting it into the Rive Droite (Right Bank) and the Rive Gauche (Left Bank). In addition, Paris is divided into twenty arrondissements (administrative districts). Each arrondissement has a name and a number. The first is called "Louvre" and is located in the very center of the city. From there, the arrondissements spiral outward clockwise through the city. The number of the arrondissement is generally indicated on the street signs.

Most stores in Paris open around 10am and close around 7:30pm, although small shops and some grocery stores close between noon and 3pm. Small neighborhood convenience stores are an exception and usually don't close until midnight. Many grocery stores and food markets are open Sunday mornings but closed on Mondays. In the traditionally Jewish neighborhoods of the Marais and Montmartre, most shops are open on Sundays. In August, many restaurants, cafés, and stores (bakeries and butchers) are closed for vacation season.

Twice a year, stores in France have clearance sales: three weeks in July/August and three weeks in January. Some good deals can be found at these sales. Check the exact dates ahead of time because if you are in town, you won't want to miss this.

MUSEUMS

With its beautiful, prestigious museums, Paris has become a paradise for museum lovers. However, when it comes to opening hours, beware—some museums are closed on Mondays, while others are closed on Tuesdays—there is generally no rhyme or reason to it. The Paris Museum Pass (www. parismuseumpass.com) offers access to more than sixty museums and monuments. A two-day pass costs €52, a four-day pass is €66, and a six-day pass is €78, although you often have to pay extra for temporary exhibits beyond the permanent collection. You can purchase one of these passes at the register of participating museums and monuments or at the tourist office at 25 Rue des Pyramides. If you'd rather not wait in line, consider buying your tickets online beforehand. Often there is a separate entrance for people with prepurchased tickets. Note that many museums offer free entrance to people from within the

European Union (EU) under the age of 26 and discounts to people with disabilities and to people over 60. On the first Sunday of the month, some museums are also open to the general public free of charge.

FRENCH FOOD CULTURE
People take their food seriously in France. The French love to eat and to talk about food. The two most important meals are le déjeuner (lunch) and le dîner (dinner). Le petit déjeuner (breakfast), on the other hand, tends to be a relatively simple affair: coffee, tea, or hot chocolate and a tartine (bread with jam) or croissant. Breakfast is eaten at home or in a café, most of which open early. In the morning, people in cafés have their coffee and croissant at the counter, which is perhaps not as comfortable as getting a table, but it is less expensive—it can sometimes be half the price. Order a café (espresso), café allongé (espresso diluted with hot water), café crème (espresso with warm milk), café au lait (espresso with cold milk), or a noisette (a small cup with a splash of cold milk). Lunch is usually eaten out, and lunch is often used to discuss business. Between 12:30pm and 2:30pm restaurants are therefore generally quite busy. A traditional French lunch consists of three courses, although you can opt for just an entrée (starter) or plat (main course). Don't forget to ask for a menu du jour or plat du jour (daily specials). In the evenings, Parisians often work late, and during the week they generally don't eat until 8pm, so restaurants don't open for dinner until around 7:30pm. On weekends restaurants don't start getting busy until after 9pm. Parisians love to eat out, so restaurants are usually packed. If you want to be sure to get a table, reserve one ahead of time. After a meal, tipping isn't necessary. If you do leave a tip, it means you were especially satisfied. Good to know: never seat yourself in a restaurant, always let the server take you to a table.

PUBLIC HOLIDAYS
In addition to Easter, Pentecost, and Ascension Day, which don't fall on specific dates, the following are official holidays in France:

January 1 > New Year's Day
May 1 > Labor Day
May 8 > Victory in Europe Day (end of WWII in 1945)

July 14 > Bastille Day (Quatorze Juillet)
August 15 > Assumption Day
November 1 > All Saint's Day
November 11 > Armistice Day (end of WWI in 1918)
December 25 > Christmas Day

On **June 21,** the evening of the summer solstice, Paris celebrates the Fête de la Musique. It is a day of musical revelry when people everywhere—in the streets, cafés, bars, concert halls, or at home—listen to and make music and dance in the streets.

From the evening of **July 13** until early in the morning of Quatorze Juillet you can dance in fire stations at the Bal des Pompiers—Firemen's Ball. Various festivities are organized throughout the city on **July 14.**

Starting in **early January,** cakes known as galettes des rois—each with a little charm baked inside—begin to appear in French bakeries. Every French family buys these cakes. According to tradition, once the cake is cut, the youngest

person at the table gets to decide who gets which piece. Whoever finds the charm then buys the next cake.

HAVE ANY TIPS?

We've put a lot of care into writing this guidebook. Yet shops and restaurants in Paris come and go regularly. We do our best to keep the walks and contact details as up to date as possible. However, if despite our best efforts there is a place you can't find, or if you have any comments or tips about this book, then please let us know. Email us at info@momedia.nl.

TRANSPORTATION

Paris is not only the City of Light; it is also a city of cars. To reduce traffic, Paris developed a reliable public transportation network that includes metros, commuter trains (RER), and buses. The same ticket can be used for all these different types of transportation. Tickets can be purchased at a ticket window or from machines in metro stations, RER stations, and RATP bus stations, which are part of Paris's public transportation system. Planning on using public transportation a lot? Buy a carnet de dix (ten tickets): this is cheaper than buying ten individual tickets.

The **metro** runs every day between 5:30am and about 1am, or 2am on Saturdays—exact times vary per station. On Sundays, metros run less frequently. Tickets are valid for one ride, and transfers are allowed, provided you stay underground. The RER is a regional commuter train that extends into the suburbs but can also be used within Paris. RER lines don't stop as frequently as the metro. The **RER** runs from 4:45am to 1am. Paris's many **buses** are also convenient, especially to get to know the city. You can find a map of metro and RER lines at the back of this book. Paris's public transportation company RATP has a free app, Bonjour Paris, which is useful.

As far as **taxi** prices go, Paris is very reasonable. It's also fairly easy to hail one of the 15,000 cabs that drive around the city. Note, however, a taxi will stop only if it is at least 165 feet (50 m) from a designated taxi stand. When both the light and the big taxi sign on the roof are illuminated, then the taxi is available, but if the big taxi sign is not on, then the taxi is occupied. You can also arrange a cab by phone: Taxis G7 (01 41276699).

BIKING

Paris is becoming increasingly more bike friendly. The city currently has some 250 miles (400 km) of pistes cyclables (bike paths). Every Sunday certain roads, such as those near the Canal Saint-Martin, are closed to cars. However, the average Parisian driver is still not accustomed to sharing the road with cyclists, so always be alert. Also, sometimes bike paths suddenly end or go over sidewalks, and pedestrians might not recognize the sound of a bike bell. So remember the word "attention" and be ready to use it to let people know you're coming.

The city has a bike share program with more than 20,000 bikes spread across 1,800 stations. It is called Vélib (www.velib.metropole.fr). You'll see the docked gray bikes and information kiosks all around town. The system is simple: use your credit card at any station's kiosk to buy a day pass or week pass, then borrow any bike from a dock with a green light. You pay based on how long your bike is out of a dock. You can put your bike back in any dock you want but be sure that the green light goes back on—otherwise it will make for a very expensive ride. The first half hour of each ride is free, the next half hour costs one euro, and from there it gets continuously more expensive. So Vélib is the least expensive for short rides. Since 2014, Paris now also has P'tit Vélib for kids ages two to eight. You'll find these bikes for kids in select spots, including Berges de Seine, the Bois de Boulogne, and Canal de l'Ourcq.

There are increasingly more opportunities in Paris to take guided bike tours. Numerous bike stores rent bikes, and tours are offered by companies such as Holland Bikes (www.hollandbikes.com), Paris Bike Tour (www.parisbiketour.net), and Paris à Vélo (www.parisvelosympa.com).

TOP 10 | SIGHTS AND MUSEUMS

1 Visit *The Thinker* in
Musée Rodin > p. 105

2 Admire the enormous clock in
Musée d'Orsay > p. 106

3 In **Le Grand Palais** there are often
beautiful exhibitions > p. 109

4 Check out impressive
photo exhibits in **Le Bal** > p. 34

5 Wander around the famous
Musée du Louvre > p. 42

6 Admire the beautiful
Fondation Louis Vuitton > p. 138

7 **Pompidou Centre** shows
contemporary art > p. 62

8 View Paris from the front
steps of **Sacré-Coeur** > p. 25

9 See groundbreaking exhibits in the
Palais de Tokyo > p. 102

10 Discover science, film,
and music in
Parc de la Villette > p. 141

TOP 10 | RESTAURANTS

TOP 10 | ON SUNDAYS

1 Start the day with breakfast and a macaron at **Ladurée** > p. 117

2 Enjoy **Marché Aligre** and drink wine at **Le Baron Rouge** > p. 141

3 Have brunch at **Le Marché des Enfants Rouges** > p. 77

4 Stroll along the **Canal Saint-Martin** and the **Bassin de la Villette** > p. 118

5 Picnic in **Parc des Buttes-Chaumont** > p. 133

6 Up for an exhibit? Go to the photo museum **MEP** > p. 64

7 Enjoy a stroll around **Luxembourg Gardens** > p. 97

8 Sip an apéro (aperitif) outside at **Café de Flore** > p. 89

9 **Le Mary Celeste** has the best cocktails > p. 70

10 Enjoy a jazzy brunch at **La Bellevilloise** > p. 135

TOP 10 — NIGHTLIFE

1 Dance under the bridge next to the Seine at **Faust** > p. 110

2 Have a French dinner at **Brasserie Barbès** > 2 Boulevard Barbès

3 Listen to jazz at **Sunset-Sunside** > 60 Rue des Lombards

4 Sip cocktails in style at **Candelaria** > 52 Rue de Saintonge

5 Let down your hair at **La Cité de la Mode et du Design** > 32 Quai d'Austerlitz

6 **L'Olympia** is a legendary concert hall > p. 57

7 Discover dance at **La Machine du Moulin Rouge** > 90 Boulevard de Clichy

8 Catch a French flick at **Cinéma Studio 28** > p. 34

9 Enjoy burlesque at **Le Crazy Horse** > 12 Avenue George V

10 Dance at the trendy **Les Bains Douches** > 7 Rue du Bourg l'Abbé

WALK **1**

BATIGNOLLES & MONTMARTRE

ABOUT THE WALK

This walk takes you through the 17th (Batignolles) and 18th (Montmartre) arrondissements. The beginning of the walk through Batignolles is particularly interesting if you've already been to Paris a few times and want to check out an
up-and-coming residential neighborhood with nice shops and hip restaurants.
Otherwise, if it's your first time in Paris, start at number 6 and just visit the artist area of Montmartre.

THE NEIGHBORHOODS

More young people and families are moving to **Batignolles,** where they can
meet up and hang out in the hip local restaurants. A very pleasant part of the
neighborhood is between the market hall and the Parc des Batignolles, where
there are many shops and cafés. Regular activities, such as antique markets,
are organized around the park.

La butte (the hill) de Montmartre, in the 18th arrondissement, stands high
above its surroundings. A century ago, this neighborhood—with its winding
streets and amazing panoramas—was still just a village outside Paris. In the late
19th century numerous artists settled here, including Cézanne, Van Gogh,
Renoir, and Toulouse-Lautrec, the last of whom immortalized the local nightlife
in his artwork. Today **Montmartre** continues to attract creative souls, and many
painters, photographers, directors, and journalists live in the neighborhood. You
can get a taste of this at **Place du Tertre.** To visit the top of the hill, you'll have
to walk up and down small streets. However, the reward is worth it. The view
from **Sacré-Coeur,** the highest point in Paris, is spectacular.

The diversity of shops and cafés makes Montmartre particularly pleasant. Street
musicians at Place des Abbesses, the non-touristy heart of the neighborhood,

WALK 1 DESCRIPTION (approx. 5.5 mi/8.7 km)

Start at the Brochant metro station on Rue Brochant. Stop and check out the market ❶. Turn right for a special restaurant ❷ or left on Rue Lemercier. Take the first street to the right, and then turn left ❸. Go right on Rue Legendre and right again on Rue Truffaut. On Rue Brochant head left toward the park ❹. Exit through the main park entrance, cross Place du Docteur F. Lobligeois and Rue Legendre to Rue des Batignolles ❺. Walk straight ahead for a nice men's shop ❻ or turn left and take Rue des Dames ❼ to Avenue de Clichy, then cross and go right. For art and coffee ❽ take a detour to the left. Otherwise, continue walking and turn left on Rue Capron. Cross the bridge over the cemetery ❾. At Rue Joseph de Maistre, head right and enjoy the panoramic view ❿. At the end of the street, turn right and head down to a famous café ⓫. Walk back and turn right on Rue Tholozé to catch a movie ⓬. Then walk back in the direction you came from and follow the road to the right onto Rue Lepic. Take the first left, then turn right onto Rue Caulaincourt. Turn right down the alley Rue J. Métivier and up the stairs to Avenue Junot ⓭ and enjoy the stunning houses and a cup of coffee ⓮ ⓯. Then take Rue Simon Dereure and, at the end, walk up the stairs to Place Dalida ⓰. Walk to Rue des Saules and turn left for a vineyard ⓱ on the left. Walk back and turn left on Rue Cortot ⓲. At the end of the street, turn left and continue until you get to Rue Lamarck, and then turn right. Turn right on Rue de la Bonne, climb the stairs, and walk to Place du Tertre ⓳. Take in the famous view from the front of Sacré-Coeur ⓴. From there, walk down and to the left. Turn left on Rue Lamarck for an Australian-style brunch ㉑ or continue on Rue Maurice Utrillo ㉒. Head down the stairs to a cultural center ㉓ and the fabric market ㉔. Cross Place Saint-Pierre and Rue Tardieu until you reach Rue des Trois Frères. Turn left and take an immediate right on Rue d'Orsel. Continue until you reach Rue des Martyrs. Turn left for a drink and a bite to eat ㉕ or right for some interesting shops down Rue des Abbesses ㉖ ㉗ and great coffee ㉘. Walk back and turn left on Rue des Martyrs ㉙ ㉚. Turn left to Rue Yvonne le Tac for a nice bookshop ㉛ or walk straight ahead to browse a vintage shop ㉜. On Rue la Vieuville, bear left to an interesting wall ㉝. Cross the square and take Rue des Abbesses. For more great food, continue up the stairs and over the square, then turn left on Rue d'Orchampt. At the end of the street, turn right down the alley ㉞ ㉟ to end at Rue Norvins.

SIGHTS & ATTRACTIONS

🔅 The beautiful, famous **Montmartre Cemetery** (Cimetière de Montmartre) dates to 1825. Many famous people have been laid to rest in this cemetery, including Émile Zola, Heinrich Heine, and Edgar Degas.
20 Avenue Rachel, 18th arr., en.parisinfo.com/paris-museum-monument/71184/ cimetiere-de-montmartre, Nov 6-March 15 Mon-Fri 8am-5:30pm, Sat 8:30am-5:30pm, Sun 9am-5:30pm, March 16-Nov 5 Mon-Fri 8am-6pm, Sat 8:30am-6pm, Sun 9am-6pm, free, Metro Place de Clichy

🔢 The beautiful blind alley **Villa Léandre** grabs your attention immediately. The English-style architecture stands out here because it is about the only place in Paris where you'll find brick homes. Previously called Villa Junot, the street was later renamed after a famous Montmartre personality—humorist Léandre.
Villa Léandre, 18th arr., Metro Lamarck Caulaincourt

🔢 **Place Dalida** is tucked away behind the Château des Brouillards and is adorned with a bust of the singer Dalida who is well loved by the French, especially in Montmartre where she lived for many years and where she passed away. Her songs can be heard often on radio throughout the neighborhood. Dalida is buried in the Montmartre cemetery.
Place Dalida, 18th arr., Metro Abbesses or Lamarck Caulaincourt

🔢 Two thousand years ago the Romans brought vineyards to Paris. At the time, wine production was a very lucrative activity. However, from the 18th century quantity steadily began to take precedence, leaving much to be desired in terms of quality. Today there are still some 2,000 vines in Montmartre: **Les Vignes de Montmartre.** You can book a wine tasting and a tour of the vineyard on the Musée de Montmartre website. During the harvest, the second weekend of October, there are street parties in Montmartre. There is music everywhere and every opportunity to taste a wine from the Paris vineyard.
Corner of Rue des Saules and Rue Saint-Vincent, 18th arr., https:// museedemontmartre.fr/evenements/visite-des-vignes-du-clos-montmartre-et-du-musee-de-montmartre, entrance to vineyard includes tour and tasting, €35, Metro Lamarck Caulaincourt

⑱ Musée de Montmartre houses a collection of works provided by the Vieux Montmartre History and Archeology Society, which was founded in 1886. The collection provides an overview of the artistic, political, and religious history of the neighborhood. Here you'll find a replica of the old town, a collection of Clignancourt porcelain, and a wonderful assortment of posters from the Golden Age of Montmartre.

12-14 Rue Cortot, 18th arr., www.museedemontmartre.fr, Mon & Wed-Sun 10am-6pm, €13, Metro Lamarck Caulaincourt

⑳ The Romano-Byzantine basilica of **Sacré-Coeur** was built to honor the Sacred Heart and ask forgiveness for the blood shed during the Franco-Prussian War. Those who dare to climb the 222 steps will be rewarded with a stunning panoramic view of Paris. But you can also take the elevator. Although the exterior is very striking, the interior is also worth a visit. The church is decorated with paintings and sculptures. Inside the dome is a large mosaic with one of the largest images in the world of Jesus Christ.

35 Rue du Chevalier de la Barre, 18th arr., www.sacre-coeur-montmartre.com, daily 6am-11pm, free, Metro Abbesses

㉟ In the 16th century, Montmartre was characterized by its many windmills. They were used to grind wheat and press grapes. Unfortunately, only a few of these windmills remain today, one of which is **Le Moulin de la Galette.** You can get a nice meal in the restaurant now located there.

83 Rue Lepic, 18th arr., www.lemoulindelagalette.fr, daily noon-10:15pm, Metro Blanche or Abbesses

FOOD & DRINK

❷ At **Coretta**, Michelin-worthy haute cuisine meets Mexican comfort food. Located on Martin Luther King Park, the restaurant is named after the freedom fighter's wife. It has a modern and stylish interior, and from the second floor you can look out over the treetops of the park. The dishes are colorful and almost like little works of art. And they taste amazing!

151 Bis, Rue Cardinet, 17th arr., tel. 01 42265555, www.restaurantcoretta.com, Tue-Sat noon-2pm & 7:30pm-10pm, lunch €29, Metro Brochant

❸ Brunch at **Les Puces des Batignolles** is so popular that the restaurant had to open a second location across the street. The meal includes a basket with croissants and jam, and a savory main course with a burger and/or eggs, plus coffee, tea, or fresh juice. Everything is served on playful, colorful dishes.
110 Rue Legendre, 17th arr., tel. 01 42266226, Mon-Fri 8am-2pm, Sat-Sun 10am-2pm, brunch €18, Metro Rome or Brochant

❼ **Les Caves Populaires** is an inviting neighborhood café and is particularly popular among students. Order a cheese platter and a glass of wine and have a nice chat with the people around you.
22 Rue des Dames, 17th arr., tel. 01 53040832, Mon-Fri 8:30am-2am, Sat 10am-2am, Sun 11am-2am, €10, Metro Rome or Place de Clichy

❿ **The Terrass Hotel** was fully renovated in 2015. On the seventh floor there is now a restaurant that offers an amazing panoramic view of the city both from inside and from outside on the terrace. You can reserve an inside table online, but they don't take reservations for the terrace.
12-14 Rue Joseph de Maistre, 18th arr., www.terrass-hotel.com, tel. 01 46067285, bar is open Tue-Sat 3:30pm-12:30am, Sun-Mon 3:30pm-11:30pm, breakfast daily 7am-10:30am, lunch Mon-Fri noon-2:30pm, dinner Tue-Sat 7pm-10:30pm, €32, Metro Blanche or Abbesses

⓫ Ever since the success of the film *Amélie,* **Café des Deux Moulins** has grown in popularity. The heroine of the movie works in this café. If you know the movie, you will recognize the place when you walk in. Enjoy a crème brûlée d'Amélie and a cup of coffee on the terrace.
15 Rue Lepic, 18th arr., www.cafedesdeuxmoulins.fr, tel. 01 42549050, Mon-Fri 7am-2am, Sat-Sun 9am-2am, €16, Metro Blanche

⓮ **Marcel** is a New York-style café on the corner of the beautiful street Villa Léandre. The menu offers primarily British and American dishes, such as eggs Benedict and blueberry pancakes. This small, dark, but good restaurant is enormously popular among locals.
1 Villa Léandre, 18th arr., www.restaurantmarcel.fr, tel. 01 46060404, Mon-Fri 10am-3pm & 6pm-10pm, Sat 10am-10pm, Sun 10am-7pm, €23, Metro Lamarck Caulaincourt

⑮ Le Très Particulier is not the easiest place to find, but once you've managed to make your way down the alley and into the courtyard of the luxurious Hotel Particulier Montmartre, you'll understand why Parisians love it so much. By day, tea is served in the charming garden and conservatory but come nighttime this spot becomes the perfect backdrop for sipping cocktails or prosecco.

23 Avenue Junot, 18th arr., https://www.hotel-particulier-montmartre.com/le-tres-particulier.html, tel. 01 53418140, bar is open daily 6pm-2am, cocktail €15, Metro Lamarck Caulaincourt

㉑ A great breakfast is easy enough to come by in Paris, but you'd be hard pressed to find anything as unique as the food at **Hardware Société.** Here, French petit déjeuner is served with an Australian twist. Enjoy coffee and any of an assortment of pastries or go all out and get a full, warm breakfast. Both sweet and savory options are sure to please your palate.

10 Rue Lamarck, 18th arr., hardwaresociete.com, tel. 01 42516903, Mon & Thurs-Sun 9:30am-4pm, €15, Metro Château Rouge

㉒ As you head down the steps from Sacré-Coeur, an inviting terrace with color-ful tables suddenly appears from behind the trees. **L'Été en Pente Douce** is a great place for a break, and it's just off the beaten tourist path.
8 Rue Paul Albert, 18th arr., lete-en-pente-douce.business.site, tel. 01 42640267, daily noon-midnight, €17.50, Metro Anvers

㉕ The retro-industrial rock 'n' roll bar **La Fourmi** is known as the place where bands like to go to warm up before taking the stage. It can also get quite busy here after performances. Grab some flyers from the bar so you know what's happening in the neighborhood. This is mainly a place to go for a drink, although the menu does offer little nibbles such as sandwiches and salads if you're hungry.
74 Rue des Martyrs, 18th arr., tel. 01 42647035, Mon-Sat 10am-midnight, drink €2.80, Metro Pigalle

㉘ "Coffee, brunch, love" is the slogan at **Sylon de Montmartre.** They serve coffee made from specially roasted beans, homemade pastries, and a delicious brunch made from organic ingredients. It's a cozy little place, perfect for a break.
4 Bis Rue Piémontési, 18th arr., www.sylondemontmartre.com, tel. 01 42575810, Mon-Fri 8:30am-5pm, Sat-Sun 10am-5pm, lunch €10, Metro Abbesses

㉞ Since the opening of **Le Coq & Fils,** it has been a huge success. The restau-rant serves only poultry, hence the name. Try the delicious chicken soup and French chicken livers or share a large chicken rôti straight out of the oven.
98 Rue Lepic, 18th arr., www.lecoq-fils.com, tel. 01 42598289, daily noon-2:30pm and 7-11:30pm, chicken to share €95, lunch €18, Metro Abbesses

SHOPPING

❶ The **Marché des Batignolles** is a covered market where you'll find many French foods, including vegetables, cheeses, meats, fish, etc. This is also the place to look for Lebanese, Morocco, African, Italian, and Spanish products. Be sure to stop by the Iranian stand in the middle of the market. Their olive-fig tapenade is unparalleled, and they'll give you a sample to prove it.

96 Bis Rue Lemercier, 17th arr., www.paris.fr/equipements/marche-couvert-batignolles-5517, Tue 9am-2pm & 4pm-8:30pm, Wed-Fri 8:30am-1pm & 4pm-8pm, Sat 8:30am-8:30pm, Sun 8:30am-2pm, Metro Brochant

❺ A visit to the cheerful and colorful **Les Petits Raffineurs** is a treat. They sell great gifts for children and unusual toys, and often these are made from ecologically friendly materials.

39 Rue des Batignolles, 17th arr., www. lespetitsraffineurs.com, Tues-Fri 11am-7:30pm, Sat 10:30am-7pm, Metro Place de Clichy

❻ **Hast** makes timeless and stylish men's wear. The concept is simple: by working with the shortest possible supply chain, Hast makes high-quality clothing for the fairest possible price. The result is a sustainable and beautiful brand. For the man who loves classy and timeless, but trendy, items.

7 Rue des Batignolles, 17th arr., www.hast.fr, Mon-Sat 11am-7:30pm, Metro Rome

㉔ **Marché Saint-Pierre** is the most famous fabric market in Paris. Enter through Dreyfus Déballage and prepare to be amazed at the enormous selection you find. Be sure to also look across the street at Tissus Reine on Place Saint-Pierre. The mini mannequins throughout the store show off the latest fabric trends.

2 Rue Charles Nodier, 18th arr., www.marchesaintpierre.com, tel. 01 46069225, Mon-Fri 10am-6:30pm, Sat 10am-7pm, Metro Anvers

㉖ At **Petite Mendigote,** you can see where French women get their style. Do you want to look utterly French à la Jane Birkin and Brigitte Bardot? Then you've come to the right place. This French brand makes romantic, feminine clothing in which, according to founder Sybille, you can go to work and to dinner wearing the same outfit.

1 Rue des Abbesses, 18th arr. www.petitemendigote.com, Mon 1pm-7pm, Tue-Fri 11am-2:15pm & 2:45pm-7pm, Sat 10:30am-7:30pm, Sun 1pm-7pm, Metro Pigalle

㉗ There's no resisting—once you set eyes on the colorful, feminine dresses at **Héroïnes,** you'll have no choice but to go in and check out the store. There are petite sizes and dresses that will steal the show at any party. The accessories are also worth checking out—shoes, feminine cufflinks, and leather belts in a variety of colors, to name a few.
7 Rue des Abbesses, 18th arr., www.heroines.fr, tel. 01 42740991, daily 11am-1pm & 2pm-10pm, Metro Abbesses

㉙ Sustainable and fair trade, that is **Ekyog.** Think playful, feminine clothing with pretty prints and bright colors. This French brand is a pioneer in the creation of sustainable fashion and proves, once again, that sustainable doesn't have to be boring.
89 Rue des Martyrs, 18th arr., www.ekyog.com, Tue-Sat 11am-2pm and 3pm-7:30pm, Sun 1pm-7:30pm, Metro Pigalle

㉚ La Chaise Longue is a cute gift shop where you can buy all kinds of fun stuff. Nice items for your home, often with a funny or unexpected twist. This shop is sure to cheer you up!
91 Rue des Martyrs, 18th arr., www.lachaiselongue.fr, Wed-Sun 10:30am-7pm, Metro Pigalle or Abbesses

㉛ Marie Rose Guarniéri's bookstore, **Librairie des Abbesses,** is something of an institution in Montmartre. It is also one of the last cultural havens in the neighborhood, which today is primarily dominated by clothing shops. There are regular readings and book presentations here.
30 Rue Yvonne le Tac, 18th arr., www.librairiedesabbesses.fr, tel. 01 46068430, Mon 11am-8pm, Tues-Sat 10am-8pm, Sun noon-8pm, Metro Abbesses

㉜ If you like thrifting clothes and looking for vintage treasures, visit **Chinemachine**. If you search well, you might find a special designer tote or coat. The lovely, international staff will be happy to assist you in your search.
100 Rue des Martyrs, 18th arr., www.chinemachinevintage.com, daily 11am-6pm, Metro Abbesses

MORE TO EXPLORE

❹ The lovely **Square des Batignolles** makes for a relaxing stop, where you can watch ducks in and around the little lake as you soak in the sun on the lawn. There's also a carousel for kids, and nearby streets such as Rue Legendre have cute shops.

Square des Batignolles, 17th arr., https://enparisinfo.com/paris-museum-monument /71291/Square-des-Batignolles, daily, free, Metro Pont Cardinet

❽ In the 1920s there was a dancehall where today you'll find **Le Bal**—one of the hottest spots in the neighborhood. The venue has an exhibition space where modern photographers and video artists display their work, and there is a store with unique art books. On weekends, the modern café serves English-style brunch.

6 Impasse de la Défense, 18th arr., www.le-bal.fr, tel. 01 44707550, Wed noon-8pm, Thurs-Sun noon-7pm, €7, Metro Place de Clichy

⓬ Pop inside at **Cinéma Studio 28** to see what is showing. This local movie theater dates to the end of the 19th century, and it still maintains much of its original character today. Artists such as Jean Cocteau and André Breton have held performances here in the past. When the weather is nice, the patio is a pleasant place for a break.

10 Rue Tholozé, 18th arr., www.cinema-studio28.com, tel. 01 46063607, see website for opening hours, €9.50, Metro Abbesses or Blanche

⓳ Montmartre was once much-loved by poets and painters alike. Perhaps that's why the busy, touristy **Place du Tertre** is nowadays always swarming with so-called artists wanting to draw your portrait. The souvenir shops and cafés on the square are also eager to cash in on the area's rich artistic past.

Place du Tertre, 18th arr., Metro Abbesses

㉓ In the 19th century, the **Halle Saint-Pierre** was the center of the fabric trade. Now the beautiful glass-and-metal construction houses the Musée d'Art Brut et

d'Art Singulier. You can come here to see temporary exhibits, go to a reading, or simply read the paper and have a bite in the charming café. Be sure to stop in at the bookstore—it has beautiful postcards.

2 Rue Ronsard, 18th arr., www.hallesaintpierre.org, Mon-Fri 11am-6pm, Sat 11am-7pm, Sun noon-6pm, exhibits €9, Metro Anvers

🌞 Behind Place des Abbesses, in a small public garden on Square Jehan Rictus, you'll find **Le Mur des Je T'aime.** On the wall, which was created in 2000, the phrase "I love you" appears 311 times in languages and dialects from around the world. You might have to look a while, but you'll eventually find English on there.

Place des Abbesses, 18th arr., www.lesjetaime.com, Metro Abbesses

WALK 2

QUARTIER DES MARTYRS, GRANDS BOULEVARDS, LOUVRE & MADELEINE

ABOUT THE WALK

This route takes you to Paris's Right Bank, namely the 9th, 1st, and 2nd arrondissements. The walk is a mix of shopping and culture. Along Rue des Martyrs and the shopping arcades there is much window shopping to be had. Along the way, there are small museums as well as the Palais Royal gardens and the Louvre where you can take in art and culture. The route starts right under Montmartre and descends to the Seine, so don't do it in reverse or you'll be in for a lot of uphill walking.

NEIGHBORHOODS

In the 9th arrondissement, the northern neighborhood between Notre-Dame de Lorette, Trinité, and Place Pigalle has been called the "golden artists' triangle." In the second half of the 19th century, it was the preferred neighborhood for artists and intellectuals, such as George Sand, Eugène Delacroix, and Frédéric Chopin. This area of the city is known for its classic architecture, with hôtels particuliers (grand residences), charming squares, quiet courtyards, and small museums. The **Rue des Martyrs** is the best-known street in the neighborhood. Here you'll find a variety of stores along with nice places to eat and drink. On Sundays this is a great area to come to for brunch among the locals.

On the Rive Droite (Right Bank) and around the **Grands Boulevards** there are many fancy shopping arcades, such as **Galerie Vivienne.** These arcades date back to the first half of the 19th century and were built to protect the wealthy from the weather while shopping. On the Grands Boulevards there are also large department stores—**Les Grands Magasins**—including Galeries Lafayette and Le Printemps. Around the square where the enormous Roman temple **La Madeleine** is located there are numerous specialty food stores and tearooms.

WALK 2 DESCRIPTION (approx. 5.8 mi/9.4 km)

Start with traditional French cuisine ❶ or go to Rue Duperré for a colorful basketball court ❷. At the end of the street are an Italian restaurant ❸ and a fun
terrace ❹. Turn left on Rue Mansart and left on Rue Blanche. Then take the first
street to the left ❺. From here take Rue Henner and turn left onto Rue la
Bruyère. Halfway down the street, turn right for a museum ❻. Otherwise continue straight to the intersection. Cross and take Rue Henry Monnier ❼ ❽.
Then take Rue Clauzel and take the first left ❾ or the second left ❿. Where Rue
des Martyrs bends, take Avenue Trudaine ⓫. At the end is a nice bar ⓬. Turn
right on Rue de Rochechouart and walk all the way down the street to the
Cadet metro station. Cross the street there and continue on Rue Cadet. Cross
Rue du Faubourg Montmartre, taste special sweets ⓭, head left for a bit, then
almost immediately right into the Passage Jouffroy Verdeau. Walk through the
shopping arcade to Boulevard de Montmartre. Turn left and then left again for a
traditional restaurant ⓮ or cross the street and continue on into the Passage
des Panoramas. Walk through the shopping arcade to Rue Vivienne, where
you'll turn left and walk to enjoy Italian food for lunch ⓯. The entrance to Galerie
Vivienne is nearby ⓰. Walk through the shopping arcade. When you exit at the
other side, cross Rue de la Banque and continue over the square in front of the
Notre-Dame-des-Victoires Basilica to Place des Victoires ⓱. From here take Rue
la Feuillade to Rue des Petits Champs for the best ramen ⓲. Go right and right
again immediately for a nice cup of coffee ⓳ or walk back a bit and turn right to
enter the beautiful Jardin du Palais Royal ⓴ ㉑ and stroll through. Exit at the
Place du Palais Royal. Cross Rue de Rivoli and head to the Louvre ㉒. Then walk
along the right side of the Louvre gardens and check out a museum and a
restaurant with a great terrace ㉓ ㉔. From here, don't go into the Tuileries
Gardens, but instead turn right on Rue des Pyramides. Take the first street to
the left, Rue Saint Honoré. Then turn right on Rue du Marché Saint-Honoré to
reach Place du Marché Saint Honoré ㉕. Continue on Rue d'Antin until you reach
Avenue de l'Opéra, then take a left to visit the Opéra ㉖. Behind this, on
Boulevard Haussmann, you'll find many of the big department stores ㉗. Walk
back and take Rue Scribe to a perfume museum ㉘ before turning right onto
Boulevard des Capucines ㉙. Walk on until you get to the church ㉚. Walk
around the church and find an informal bistro and deli ㉛ ㉜ ㉝ ㉞.

SIGHTS & ATTRACTIONS

❺ The building that now houses the **Musée de la Vie Romantique** was a meeting place for Paris's Romantic artists during the 19th century. This hôtel particulier was the home and studio of painter Ary Scheffer. His own works tell us all about this period, as do memorabilia from writer George Sand. The tearoom and the idyllic garden are especially romantic.

16 Rue Chaptal, 9th arr., museevieromantique.paris.fr, Tues-Sun 10am-6pm, garden April-Oct, free entrance to permanent collection, temporary exhibits start at €7, Metro Blanche

❻ Artist Gustave Moreau (1826-1898) was considered part of the Symbolism movement. His former home and studio now house the **Musée National Gustave Moreau.** His unique paintings cover the walls from floor to ceiling, and numerous sketches and watercolors are contained in glass cases.

14 Rue de la Rochefoucauld, 9th arr., www.musee-moreau.fr, Mon & Wed-Sun 10am-6pm, €7, Metro Trinité or St.-Georges

🖼 The building that is home to the **Louvre Museum (Musée du Louvre)** has served many purposes—from medieval fortress to imperial palace. In 1793 Napoleon decided to open the palace to the public, and the Louvre has since become the richest, most visited museum in the world. There is so much to see that, even if you were to just fleetingly glance at all the art, it would still take a full day or two. Tip: avoid the lines and buy your tickets online.

34-36 Quai du Louvre, 1st arr., www.louvre.fr, Mon & Wed-Sun 9am-6pm, €17, Metro Palais Royal-Musée du Louvre

🖼 The focus of the **Musée des Arts Décoratifs** is applied art: design, interior design, advertising, graphic design, and fashion. The permanent collection includes interesting Art Nouveau and Art Deco pieces and modern furniture from the 20th century. The museum also has temporary exhibits. From the top floor of the building, the view is amazing out over the Jardin des Tuileries.

107-111 Rue de Rivoli, 1st arr., www.lesartsdecoratifs.fr, Tues-Wed & Fri-Sun 11am-6pm, Thurs 11am-9pm, €14, Metro Palais Royal-Musée du Louvre

26 **L'Opéra Garnier** was built between 1862 and 1875. The wedding cake—as the building is affectionately known—was designed by Charles Garnier. The opulent edifice combines a mix of styles and is adorned with hundreds of statues. During the day, it is possible to tour the building. Of course, the best option is to see a performance there.

8 Rue Scribe, 9th arr., www.operadeparis.fr, daily 10am-4:30pm, €14 (Exhibition Periods), audio guide & multimedia visit €5, with iPad €12, Metro Opéra

28 The French are known to be proud of their products. So it's not surprising that there is an entire museum dedicated to Fragonard, a perfumery from the southern town of Grasse known for its flowery fragrances. **Musée du Parfum Fragonard** is in a beautiful old building that dates to 1860, and much of the museum's decorations date from that time as well. A multilingual guide will give you a tour, and you will be able to check out a private perfume collection. Extend the olfactory pleasure beyond your visit and buy your favorite fragrance to take home.

9 Rue Scribe, 9th arr., musee-parfum-paris.fragonard.com, Mon-Sat 10am-7pm, free, Metro Opéra

With **La Madeleine,** Napoleon had wanted to make a Roman temple to the glory of his army. Building began in 1764, but by the time it was finished in 1842 there was no longer a need for a monument that celebrated Napoleon's fallen soldiers. In the end, the building became a church that has a daily mass.

Place de la Madeleine, 8th arr., www.eglise-lamadeleine.com, daily 9:30am-7pm, free, Metro Madeleine

FOOD & DRINK

❶ The concept of **Bouillon Pigalle** is both simple and brilliant: traditional French cooking done on a large scale so that prices are low and the quality of the food is high. Don't be put off by the long line: the skilled staff will guide you to a table as quickly as possible. You won't find a less expensive meal in Paris.

22 Boulevard de Clichy, 18de arr., www.bouillonpigalle.com, tel. 01 42596931, daily noon-midnight, €10, Metro Pigalle

❸ The Instagrammable restaurant **Pink Mamma** is a feast for the eyes, but it's mainly known for its delicious Italian food. Pasta, pizza, and the specialty of the house—a giant Florentine steak that weighs a whopping 800 grams. There's a speakeasy in the basement where you can drink delicious cocktails. Even though the place has four floors, there is often a line outside, so come early or make reservations.

20 Bis Rue de Douai, 9th arr., www.bigmammagroup.com/en/trattorias/pink-mamma, Mon-Wed noon-2:30pm & 6:45pm-10:45pm, Thurs-Fri noon-2:15pm & 6:45pm-11pm, Sat noon-3:15pm & 6:45pm-11pm, Sun noon-3:15pm & 6:45pm-10:45pm, €18, Metro Pigalle

❹ **Le Dépanneur** is located on one of the nicest squares in the Pigalle neighborhood, and its sunny terrace is a perfect place to pass the time. The restaurant got its start as the city's first organic food truck, and traces of its earlier incarnation can still be found in the food it serves today—namely organic burgers and tacos. Be sure to order one of their delicious cocktails to go with your meal.
27 Rue Pierre Fontaine, 9th arr., www.ledepanneur-pigalle.com, tel. 01 48744874, daily noon-2am, €15, Metro Blanche

❾ The restaurant at the small, chic **Hôtel Amour** is a good place to come for a drink at the bar, lunch, or a romantic dinner. With a little luck, you will be able to find a table in the charming inner courtyard. They serve a delicious brunch on the weekends. Choose from a variety of tasty options, including marinated salmon, eggs Benedict, salads, and burgers.
8 Rue Navarin, 9th arr., www.hotelamourparis.fr, tel. 01 48783180, daily 8am-2am, €22, Metro Pigalle

❿ From the day it first opened, **Le Pantruche** has been hugely popular—and for good reason. Classic, refined French cuisine is served here with originality and professionalism. The interior is simple yet stylish, and the quality is perfect for the price. Unfortunately, the restaurant is open only on weekdays.
3 Rue Victor Massé, 9th ar.r, tel. 01 48785560, www.lapantruchoise.com, Mon-Fri 12:30pm-2:30pm & 7:30pm-9:30pm, lunch €19, dinner €38, Metro Pigalle

⓫ If you fancy a good cup of coffee, head to **KB Café.** The baristas are not only very skilled at making a strong cappuccino or espresso, but they also roast their own beans and bake their own cakes. If you can't get enough of the house blend, you can buy the beans onsite or order them online.
53 Avenue Trudaine, 9th arr., www.kbcoffeeroasters.com, tel. 01 5692141241, Mon-Fri 7:45am-6:30pm, Sat-Sun 9am-6:30pm, coffee €4.50, Metro Pigalle

⓬ In the mood for a drink? **Dunkerque** is one of the hottest bars in Pigalle. There is an extensive drinks menu with a good selection of different types of rum, special cocktails, and craft beers. Order some hors d'oeuvres to go with

your drinks, and you've got the perfect recipe for a great night out. This is also a nice spot for lunch or dinner.

1 Avenue Trudaine, 9th arr., cafedunkerque.com, tel. 01 42811134, daily 8am-2am, €19, Metro Anvers

14 The legendary **Bouillon Chartier** has been around since 1896 and is something of an institution in Paris. The restaurant's concept has always remained the same: good food for a good price, served up with outstanding service. Now, after all these years, it is still popular. They don't take reservations here, so the line out front continuously grows as the evening progresses. Tip: come here for an early dinner, and you're likely to be seated immediately. The extensive menu offers a variety of typical French dishes, and the large dining area—with lots of glass and mirrors—is a historic monument.

7 Rue du Faubourg Montmartre, 9th arr., www.bouillon-chartier.com, tel. 01 47708629, daily 11:30am-11pm, €15, Metro Grands Boulevards

⓯ Located in what was once a Jean Paul Gaultier store is the stylish **Daroco.** The interior is gorgeous: in a space with high ceilings, guests dine at green marble tables and are waited on by charming staff in Breton-striped shirts. Here they serve delicious food from the open kitchen, including brick oven pizza and fancy pasta dishes. Daroco may not be the least expensive Italian food, but it certainly is some of the best.
6 Rue Vivienne, 2nd arr., www.daroco.fr, tel. 01 42219371, daily noon-midnight, main course €20, menu €48, Metro Bourse

⓲ Nearby the Palais Royal, at Rue Sainte-Anne and Rue des Petits Champs, you'll find the heart of "Little Tokyo." This area is frequented by Japanese expats hankering for a taste of home, many of whom don't mind waiting in line at **Kotteri Ramen Naritake** for traditional Japanese ramen soup. The ramen can be served with extra fat (gita gita) or made low-fat (sappari), depending on your taste. Be sure to order some crispy gyoza, too, while you're here.
31 Rue des Petits Champs, 1st arr., tel. 01 42860383, Mon & Wed-Sun 11:30am-3pm & 6:30pm-10pm, €10, Metro Pyramides

⓳ **Télescope Café** is a minimalistic and trendy little café. On the menu are different types of coffee, tea, and some pastries. Their banana bread is fantastic! It's a nice place for a break or take something to go and sit at the adjacent Palais Royal.
5 Rue Villédo, 1st arr., tel. 01 42613314, Mon-Fri 8:30am-3pm, coffee €4, Metro Pyramides

㉑ In the garden of the Palais Royal you'll find the cozy coffee bar **Café Kitsuné.** Sit and enjoy your coffee and cake at the counter or get your drink to go and stroll through the galleries and past the high-end shops of the Palais Royal. When the weather is nice, the green chairs near the fountain are a great place to sit and recoup.
51 Galerie de Montpensier, 1st arr., www.maisonkitsune.com, tel. 01 40156231, daily 10am-6:30pm, coffee €4, Metro Palais Royal-Musée du Louvre

24 The terrace at the modern **LouLou** is just off the beaten path taken by tourists through the Jardin des Tuileries. It's a great place to come for a delicious, elegant lunch with a view out over the gardens. The terrace gets full sun, but there are enough umbrellas to provide ample shade. From the terrace you can even see the Eiffel Tower in the distance. It's the perfect spot for a romantic date.

107 Rue de Rivoli, 1st arr., loulou-paris.com, tel. 01 42604196, Mon-Fri noon-2:30pm and 7pm-11pm, Sat-Sun 12:30pm-2:30pm & 7pm-11pm, €30, Metro Palais Royal-Musée du Louvre

25 There are a variety of places to eat at the Place du Marché de Saint-Honoré, from simple to stylish. One of the more upscale places is **L'Absinthe.** The food here is great: beautiful fish and meat dishes served in a classic, charming interior.

24 Place du Marché Saint-Honoré, 1st arr., www.restaurantabsinthe.com, tel. 01 49269004, Mon-Thurs noon-2:15pm & 7pm-10:15pm, Fri noon-2:15 & 7pm-10:45pm, Sat 7pm-10:45pm, €22, Metro Tuileries

31 **Paris London** is one of those typical bistros you'll find only in Paris. Cozy, informal, with a terrace that overlooks the imposing church of La Madeleine. With a menu full of French classics, such as croque monsieur and sirloin steak, mixed with burgers and pizzas, Paris London is the perfect place to relax with a nice lunch, casual dinner, or the favorite activity of Parisians: an apéro with a cheese plate.

10 Place de la Madeleine, 8th arr., www.parislondon.paris, tel. 01 47423392, daily 7am-2am, €10, Metro Madeleine

SHOPPING

7 **Pois Plume** is a cute shop for the tiniest tots and their mamas. They have clothes, decorations for the baby's room, and toys. The collection has been very carefully put together, and the colors, fabrics, and clothes will bring a smile to your face. You might not be able to leave without a cute little something for someone.

4 Rue Henry Monnier, 9th arr., www.poisplume.com, Tues-Sat 11am-7:30pm, Sun 12:30pm-7pm, Metro St.-Georges

8 Exactly how **Juju S'amuse** is able time and again to put together such great clothing collections is a mystery. But Juju does, and its success is reflected in the fact that, in addition to having boutiques in Paris, it now also has a store in New York. Here you'll find colorful, one-of-a-kind items for the fashion-conscious woman.
3 Rue Henry Monnier, 9th arr., www.jujusamuse.com, Mon-Sat 10:30am-7:30pm, Sun 3pm-7pm, Metro St.-Georges

13 **À la Mère de Famille** has been around since 1761 and might be the oldest candy story in Paris. It sells pastries, chocolates, and candies. The façade is an eye-catcher, and some of the cans in the shop window are more than a few decades old.
35 Rue du Faubourg Montmartre, 9th arr., www.lameredefamille.com, Mon-Sat 9:30am-8pm, Sun 10am-7:30pm, Metro Le Peletier

27 The large department stores collectively referred to as **Les Grands Magasins** are all right next to each other. The best known is Galeries Lafayette, with its beautiful glass and metal dome. Less touristy is Le Printemps. Le Citadium sells the latest styles in streetwear.
40 Boulevard Haussman, 9th arr., www.galerieslafayette.com, Mon-Sat 10am-8pm, Sun 11am-8pm, Metro Chaussée d'Antin la Fayette

32 At **La Maison de la Truffe** almost everything smells like truffles. The restaurant serves an omelet with sliced truffle. In the giftshop there is truffle butter, chips, and olives. It's for foodies and enthusiasts!
19 Place de la Madeleine, 8th arr., www.maison-de-la-truffe.com, shop is open Mon-Sat 10am-11pm, restaurant is open Mon-Sat noon-10:30pm, Metro Madeleine

33 You'll find the most luxurious tasty treats at **Fauchon,** founded in 1886. There are countless gourmet items, a heavenly cake shop, a tearoom, a deli, and a wine cellar.
30 Place de la Madeleine, 8th arr., www.fauchon.com, daily 8am-10am & noon-9:30pm, Metro Madeleine

㉞ Since 1747, **Maille** has been about one product: mustard. Here you'll find the most unique flavors and colors of mustard, from traditional mustard with honey or nuts, to red mustard with berries and green mustard with herbs. There is also a nice selection of oils and vinegars made with mustard. This true French product is a nice complement to many of the other delicious French treats you can buy around La Madeleine.

6 Place de la Madeleine, 8th arr., www.maille.com, Mon-Sat 10am-7pm, Metro Madeleine

MORE TO EXPLORE

❷ This basketball court is a striking, colorful surprise among the typical Parisian buildings. **Playground Duperré** is accessible to everyone and gets a new look every year, often designed by prominent fashion designers. Have yourself a fun photo moment!

22 Rue Duperré, 9th arr., open daily, free, Metro Pigalle

⑯ Paris is full of shopping arcades. The glass-covered halls were built during the 19th century under the supervision of the architect Georges-Eugène Haussmann, who was likely inspired by the architecture of Arabian souks. The best preserved and perhaps most lively of these arcades is **Galerie Vivienne,** built in 1823 and decorated in Empire style. Walk through the passage to discover its many quaint boutiques and restaurants.

5 Rue de la Banque, 4 Rue des Petits-Champs, 6 Rue Vivienne, 2nd arr., www.galerie-vivienne.com, daily 9am-8pm, Metro Bourse

⑰ **Place des Victoires** has been forgotten in Paris. This round square was built in 1684 to encircle a statue of Louis XIV and offers a respite from tourists. On numerous occasions throughout history the statue has been destroyed, but each time it has been replaced. Many famous fashion brands have stores here, so there is good shopping to be had.

Place des Victoires, 2nd arr., Metro Bourse or Sentier

28 Since 1986, Daniel Buren's black-and-white columns have been adding a bit of extra pep to the stately palace garden **Jardin du Palais Royal,** delivering a surprising contrast between old and new. The small garden is a popular picnic spot. Nearby shopping arcades house a variety of stores. Head to Serge Lutens for perfume, Stella McCartney for feminine clothes with a British twist, Pierre Hardy for high-fashion shoes, and Journal Standard de Luxe for good-looking basics. Along the way, stop at any of the fantastic terraces and soak up the Parisian vibe.

2 Place Colette, 1st arr., palais-royal.monuments-nationaux.fr, daily Oct-March 8am-8:30pm, April-Sept 8am-10:30pm, free, Metro Palais Royal-Musée du Louvre

29 The renowned Olympia theater was established in 1888 by Joseph Oller, founder of the Moulin Rouge, and is the oldest theater in Paris. Its iconic red façade dates to the 19th century and is a real eye-catcher on the Boulevard des Capucines. Countless celebrities have performed here, including the Beatles, Rolling Stones, David Bowie, and Céline Dion. **L'Olympia** is also well known as the place where Édith Piaf rose to fame and where she gave her last performance just months before her death. Check the website for current shows.

28 Boulevard des Capucines, 9th arr., www.olympiahall.com, see website for opening hours, Metro Opéra

WALK 3

LES HALLES & LE MARAIS

ABOUT THE WALK

This route is on the Right Bank and takes you through the 1st, 3rd, and 4th arrondissements. The walk is not ideal for Saturdays when many of the stores and restaurants in this traditionally Jewish neighborhood are closed. Take the time to stop regularly at a sidewalk café and take in everything around you. It's easy to spend an entire day here walking around and enjoying all the things you come across—hidden streets, unexpected squares, sidewalk cafés, and interesting shops.

THE NEIGHBORHOODS

Les Halles and the **Marais** are adjoining neighborhoods on the Right Bank. Les Halles was previously home to a covered market. Around the market were restaurants where merchants could eat hearty stews. In 1969 Paris's largest food market moved to the suburbs and, against protest, the covered market was torn down. In 1979 an underground shopping center called Forum des Halles was built in its place. The character of the neighborhood changed, rents climbed, and many residents were forced to move away. Today few of the original restaurants in the area remain. The neighborhood is currently undergoing complete renovation.

Another building that has changed the area is the **Pompidou Centre** (Centre Pompidou). When it opened in 1977, this center for contemporary art was the target of a lot of criticism because of its distinctive exterior with scaffolding and air ducts. Today, however, the building is now an integral part of the city scape. The area surrounding the Pompidou is almost entirely closed to cars and is brimming with stores. Paris's **Hôtel de Ville** is also in the neighborhood. This beautiful, stately building is the heart of the city. Rue de Rivoli is a perfect place to go shopping at all the typical French retail chains.

WALK 3 DESCRIPTION (approx. 5.75 mi/9.3 km)

From the Étienne Marcel metro station, take Rue de Turbigo and turn right on Rue Montmartre ❶. There are nice shops on Rue du Jour. Continue on Rue Montmartre ❷, then take Rue Tiquetonne ❸ to Rue Montorgueil ❹, where you turn left. Continue onto Rue des Petits Carreaux for a Michelin-starred restaurant ❺. Walk back and turn left on Rue Saint-Sauveur and right on Rue Dussoubs. Turn left on Rue Tiquetonne, then right on Rue Saint-Denis, and then left. You'll end up at Rue Étienne Marcel. Continue straight to Rue Beaubourg. Turn left and left again on Rue Gravilliers ❻, or turn right and left on Impasse Berthaud ❼. Take a break in a special garden ❽. Walk back and onto Rue Rambuteau. To the left is the Pompidou Centre ❾ ❿. Walk past the fountain to Rue du Renard and turn right. Continue until you get to the Hôtel de Ville ⓫. Take Rue du Temple and then the second street to the right ⓬. Then turn right on Rue des Archives and take a left on Rue de la Verrerie ⓭. Continue on Rue de la Verrerie and turn left on Rue du Bourg Tibourg. At the end of the street turn right and walk until you see the green facade of a bar ⓮. Go left and take the first right on Rue des Rosiers ⓯. Miznon is on the first street to the right ⓰. Walk to the other end of Rue des Rosiers ⓱ and turn right on Rue Pavée ⓲. Cross the street and at the St.-Paul metro station take Rue de Fourcy to ⓳. Continue until you reach Rue Charlemagne, then turn left for a small village in the city ⓴. At the end of the street turn left, then right on Rue Saint-Antoine. Turn left on Rue de Birague to Place des Vosges ㉑. Walk under the arch and take the first street on the right, Rue Roger Verlomme. Here you'll find a small French restaurant ㉒. Go left and then left again on Rue Saint-Gilles, then take the first left and then the first right. Turn left on Rue de Turenne. Turn right onto Rue des Francs Bourgeois ㉓. Continue straight, then make a right on to Rue Elzevir, where you can visit Musée Cognacq-Jay ㉔. Turn left on Rue de la Quartre Fils and then right on Rue Charlot. Take the second right onto Rue de Poitou and then the first left for a special concept store ㉕. Turn left at Rue de Bretagne ㉖, then take the second right ㉗ ㉘. Turn left on Rue Perrée, Walk past the Square du Temple and take Rue Paul Dubois to the right ㉙. From there, Rue Dupetit Thouars ㉚ will take you to Rue de Franche Comté. At the square, take the first street to the right. Then follow Rue de Normandie to the intersection with Rue de Turenne. Go diagonally left to Rue Froissart ㉛. Turn right on Boulevard Beaumarchais toward Merci ㉜, The Frankie Shop ㉝, and Maison Plisson ㉞.

SIGHTS & ATTRACTIONS

❶ Due to a lack of funds, the construction of **Église Saint-Eustache** took more than one hundred years—from 1532 to 1637. During this time styles changed, and that is reflected in the mixture of Gothic and Renaissance styles. The basic structure of the church is similar to that of Notre-Dame. The building has very tall ceilings, the inside is light, and it is ornately decorated. Famous figures including Richelieu, Molière, and Madame de Pompadour were baptized here. One thing that might surprise you is the Keith Haring triptych, which is wonderfully unexpected!

2 Impasse Saint-Eustache, www.saint-eustache.org, Mon-Fri 9:30am-7pm, Sat 10am-7:15pm, Sun 9am-7:15pm, free, Metro Les Halles

❾ **Pompidou Centre**—called "Beaubourg" by the political left—was designed by architects Renzo Piano and Richard Rogers. The building was initially highly criticized when it opened in 1977 but quickly became an important Parisian landmark. The museum's permanent collection is comprised of more than 1,400 works of art. In addition, there are numerous temporary exhibitions, as well as film screenings and conferences. Don't miss the bookshop and be sure to go up to the top for a fantastic view of the city.

Place Georges Pompidou, www.centrepompidou.fr, Mon & Wed-Sun 11am-9pm, €14, view only €5, Metro Hôtel de Ville

⓫ For centuries the **Hôtel de Ville de Paris** has been the center of political life in Paris. During the monarchy, the great square out front was the scene of public executions. In 1871, the Communards (supporters of the revolutionary government, the Paris Commune) set the building ablaze. Afterward, it was fully restored according to its original design. In a hall on the side of the building there are often nice, temporary exhibits, which you can access via the side entrance.

Place de l'Hôtel de Ville, 4th arr., www.paris.fr/pages/visiter-l-hotel-de-ville-2316, tours by reservation, free, Metro Hôtel de Ville

⓲ The **Synagogue Agudath Hakehilot** was built in 1914 and designed by Art Nouveau architect Hector Guimard, who also designed the green cast-iron

metro entrances. During World War II, Germans bombed the synagogue, but it was later restored. Today it is a national monument.

10 Rue Pavée, 4th arr., not open to the public, Metro St.-Paul

The **MEP**—Maison Européenne de la Photographie—is located in a renovated hotel. The museum's collection includes works from big names such as Helmut Newton, Martin Parr, and Sarah Moon. There is no permanent exhibition—all exhibitions are temporary. The library on the ground floor is also worth a visit.

5-7 Rue de Fourcy, 4th arr., www.mep-fr.org, Wed & Fri 11am-8pm, Thurs 11am-10pm, Sat-Sun 10am-8pm, €10, Metro St.-Paul or Pont Marie

Musée Cognacq-Jay is an unknown but wonderful museum. Here you can see the private collection of Ernest Cognacq and his wife, Marie-Louise Jaÿ, which they collected between 1900 and 1925. This museum is for anyone who loves paintings, drawings, porcelain, and furniture from the 18th century.

8 Rue Elzévir, 3rd arr., www.museecognacqjay.paris.fr, Tues-Sun 10am-6pm, free entrance to permanent collection, Metro St.-Paul or Chemin Vert

FOOD & DRINK

② **Comptoir de la Gastronomie** began its épicerie fine, or gourmet store, at the end of the 19th century, selling traditional products such as foie gras and smoked fish. In the restaurant, they serve regional French fare such as Burgundy-style escargots, duck confit, foie gras with honey, and crème brûlée. Each dish is paired with a delicious wine, which the staff will gladly advise you on.

34 Rue Montmartre, 1st arr., www.comptoirdelagastronomie.com, tel. 01 42333132, restaurant open Tue-Sat noon-2:30pm & 7pm-10:30pm, store Mon-Sat 9am-8pm, €20, Metro Les Halles

⑤ **Frenchie** opened its doors in 2009 and has since become a household name in Paris. In 2019 it was awarded a Michelin star. The kitchen is run by Gregory Marchand, who earned the nickname "Frenchie" in Jamie Oliver's kitchens. On the changing menu are dishes with French roots and an international twist. Reservations are recommended, but don't worry if you haven't managed to get a table. Frenchie also has a nice wine bar with a good selection of wines. Or get a lunch to go.

5 Rue du Nil, 2nd arr., www.frenchie-restaurant.com, tel. 01 40399619, Mon-Wed 6pm-10pm, Thurs-Fri noon-2pm & 6pm-10pm, tasting menu €115, Metro Sentier

⑥ Restaurant **Le Derrière** is hidden away on a small square near two other nice places from the same owner: 404, a Moroccan restaurant, and Andy Whaloo, which serves good cocktails. Le Derrière has done its best to create a unique dining environment. Each seating area is different, but they're all intended to make you feel at home. So, for example, you can get a table in "the bedroom," where several seats are on an actual bed. This is somewhere you come for the experience—the food itself is unexceptional. The Sunday brunch buffet is a good suggestion.

69 Rue des Gravilliers, 3rd arr., derriere-resto.com, tel. 01 44619195, Wed-Sat noon-2:30pm & 7:30pm-11pm, Sun noon-4pm & 7:30pm-11pm, €30, Sunday brunch €39, Metro Arts et Metiers

7 **Le Hangar** is tucked away in a small side street. This classic French bistro is a secret among locals. Think French classics like foie gras and duck confit, all served without any fuss. There is friendly service and an extensive wine menu. If you like to taste authentic French food, this is the place.
12 Impasse Berthaud, 3rd arr., tel. 01 42745544, Tue-Sat noon-2:30pm & 6:45pm-11pm, €20, Metro Rambuteau

10 Philippe Starck designed the modern decor at the trendy **Georges**. The restaurant is on the top floor of the Pompidou Centre and has a fantastic view out over the city. Of course, this is incorporated in the price tag. The wait staff is a team of models—everything down to the very last detail here is beautiful.
Centre Pompidou, 4th arr., restaurantgeorgesparis.com, tel. 01 44784799, Mon & Wed-Sun noon-2am, €38, Metro Rambuteau

13 From the outside, the bistro **Les Mauvais Garçons** stands out, thanks to its green facade. The inside is lower key with small tables, but the food is amazing French fare influenced by southern cuisine from Lyon. Starters include dishes such as camembert grillé and gratinée à l'oignon, main courses such as boeuf bourguignon and magret de canard, and desserts such as tarte à la praline rose. Everything tastes just as delicious as it sounds!
4 Rue des Mauvais Garçons, 4th arr., tel. 01 42727497, daily 11am-11pm, €24, Metro Hôtel de Ville

14 **Au Petit Fer à Cheval** in the Marais is a true classic. The café gets its name from its horseshoe-shaped bar made of zinc. Outside is a small terrace that is an ideal spot for people watching because it's on a busy street. The kitchen is open nonstop from noon to 1:15 am—a real rarity in Paris. So come here any day for a late lunch.
30 Rue Vieille du Temple, 4th arr., www.cafeine.com, tel. 01 42724747, daily 9am-2am, €15, Metro Hôtel de Ville or St.-Paul

16 At **Miznon** you can get the best pitas in town. Miznon is Hebrew for "buffet." Here you order at the bar, choosing from the sandwiches written on the chalkboard, and all the ingredients then go into your pita. There's plenty to

choose from. Try the mouth-watering lamb kebab, boeuf bourguignon, carrot ratatouille, or fresh marinated tuna. Prefer something sweet? Try a banana-chocolate pita. You can sit and eat at the bar or at the tables in the dining area.

22 Rue des Écouffes, 4th arr., www.miznonparis.com, tel. 01 42748358, Mon-Thu & Sun noon-11pm, Fri noon-4pm, €13, Metro St.-Paul

17 You could easily spend the entire afternoon at tearoom **Le Loir dans la Théière.** Sink into one of the comfortable armchairs and enjoy a pot of tea and an indescribably delicious tarte au citron meringué or a slice of any of the other freshly baked tarts.

3 Rue des Rosiers, 4th arr., leloirdanslatheiere.com, tel. 01 42729061, daily 9am-7:30pm, lunch €18, Metro St.-Paul

22 For a traditional French meal, **Chez Janou** is the place to go. This charming bistro serves typical Provençal fare, such as brandade de morue (salt cod and potato puree), ratatouille, and lavender crème brûlée. Inside, the tables are very close together, as is the case at most French bistros, but outside on the terrace is a particularly nice place to sit.

2 Rue Roger Verlomme, 3rd arr., www.chezjanou.com, tel. 01 42722841, Mon-Sat noon-2am, Sun noon-10pm, main course €22, Metro Chemin Vert

28 True to its name, **Paris New York** serves up American-style hamburgers. Unlike most other burger joints in Paris, this place has a modern and fresh interior, and the burgers are high quality. Classic films are projected onto the wall of the top floor. And by Paris standards, prices aren't bad, either: 16 euros for a burger, fries, and a drink.

1 Rue Perrée, 3rd arr., www.pnyhamburger.com, tel. 01 47701524, daily noon-5pm & 7pm-11:30pm, €15, Metro Temple

30 Parisians are huge fans of brunch. One of the most popular places in the Marais is hip **Season**. On the extensive menu you will find sweet as well as savory dishes, with many vegetarian or vegan options. This place is especially crowded on Sundays, and since you cannot make a reservation, we recommend you come here early.

1 Rue Charles-François Dupuis, 3rd arr., www.season-paris.com, season, tel. 09 67175297, Mon 11am-7pm, Tue-Sat 10am-8pm, Sun 11am-7pm, €10, Metro Temple

㉛ Stop by **Le Mary Céleste** for a break at the big wooden bar in front of the large, open windows. During oyster season (from September to April), come here to share a plate of oysters. Or choose a dish off the menu, which changes daily, and end the night with a cocktail.

1 Rue Commines, 3rd arr., www.lemaryceleste.com, tel. 09 80729883, Mon-Fri noon-3pm & 6pm-2am, Sat-Sun noon-2am, cocktail €12, oysters €2-5 each, Metro Filles de Calvaire

㉞ Restaurant, butcher, cheese shop, and wine store—**Maison Plisson** is all of this and much more, making it a must visit for all foodies. It has been hugely successful since opening at this address in 2014. The space is divided in two, with a small supermarket to the right, which offers fresh, high-quality produce. To the left is a restaurant where chef Bruno Doucet uses his magic to transform these very products into delicious meals.

93 Boulevard Beaumarchais, 3rd arr., www.lamaisonplisson.com, tel. 01 71181909, Mon-Sat 8:30am-9pm, Sun 8:30am-8pm, main course €18, Metro Chemin Vert

SHOPPING

❸ New and trendy brands mix with vintage at concept store **Kiliwatch**, and you can find it all under one roof. There is a large selection of clothing and accessories for both men and women. Do not expect bargains here but rather an extensive, well-curated selection of fashion items.

64, Rue Tiquetonne, 2nd arr., www.kiliwatch-paris.com, Mon 10:30am-7pm, Tues-Sat 10:30am-7:30pm, Metro Étienne Marcel

⓬ **Fleux** is a super fun concept store. The store has several locations on the street—most are big, and several occupy multiple buildings. Some of the

stores are connected by a courtyard. On offer are a variety of nice items for the home and fun games and gadgets for kids by French and international designers. Around Christmas and other gift-giving periods, the store can get very busy.

39 Rue Sainte-Croix de la Bretonnerie, 4th arr., www.fleux.com, Mon-Sat 11am-8pm, Sun 1:15pm-7:30pm, Metro Hôtel de Ville

㉓ Nearly everyone in France, young and old alike, has a pair of Bensimon sneakers in their closet. The beloved concept store **Home Autour du Monde** sells them in all styles and sizes. In addition, the store carries the Bensimon clothing line—not to mention a great selection of furniture, things for the home, and nice gift ideas.

8 Rue des Francs Bourgeois, 3rd arr., www.bensimon.com, Mon-Sat 11am-7pm, Sun 1pm-7pm, Metro Chemin Vert

㉕ The concept store **Tom Greyhound,** originally from Korea, is tucked down a side street off the bustling, terrace-filled Rue de Bretagne. Tom Greyhound is known among locals for its unique, modern interior and is a source of inspiration. The racks are filled with a mix of some of the most exclusive, modern, and progressive brands. The store also has a nice selection of accessories and lifestyle products.

19 Rue de Saintonge, 3rd arr., www.tomgreyhound.com, Mon-Sat 11am-7pm, Metro St.-Sébastien Froissart

㉗ **Empreintes** is a type of store you won't come across very often in Paris. Its size alone is impressive: nearly 6,500 square feet (604 sq. meters) divided over four floors. This concept store specializes in handicraft objects and includes an extensive collection of kitchenware, jewelry, furniture, and artwork. Prices range anywhere from 20 euros to 10,000 euros, so there's sure to be something here for everyone.

5 Rue de Picardie, 3rd arr., www.empreintes-paris.com, Tues-Sat 11am-1pm & 2pm-7pm, Metro Temple

㉙ Close to Place de la République is **0fr**, Paris's most avant-garde bookshop. The store is particularly popular among fashion lovers and art aficionados,

thanks to its large collection of art and fashion magazines. They also have a good selection of photography books. In addition to being a bookshop, 0fr is also an independent publisher and an art gallery, and the friendly staff is always happy to provide information about 0fr's monthly exhibitions.
20 Rue Dupetit-Thouars, 3rd arr., daily 10am-8pm, Metro Temple

32 Merci is a concept store with a do-good dimension—a portion of profits go to a foundation that funds, among other things, school meals for kids in Madagascar. The mini department store has a unique, thoughtful collection of clothing, decorations, kitchen items, and furniture. The underlying trend here is hip and sustainable. In the basement, La Cantine Merci is a popular lunch spot. On the ground floor there is also the Used Book Café, and one door down is the Merci Cinema Café. Further down the street, at number 91, is their pizzeria Grazie.
111 Boulevard Beaumarchais, 3rd arr., www.merci-merci.com, Mon-Sat 11am-7:30pm, Sun 11am-7pm Metro St.-Sébastien Froissart

33 The **Frankie Shop** is one of those stores where you want everything. Here you will find clothing that embodies the Parisian style: oversized jackets, jeans, tops, and beautiful, high-quality accessories.
14 Rue Saint-Claude, 3rd arr., www.thefrankieshop.com, Mon-Fri noon-7pm, Sat 11am-7pm, Sun 2pm-6pm, Metro St.-Sébastien Froissart

MORE TO EXPLORE

4 Rue Montorgueil is situated between Les Halles and les Grands Boulevards and it's a village in the middle of Paris. It is lively and home to a few of the best culinary specialty shops the city has to offer. Pop into the award-winning La Maison Stohrer for patisserie, La Fermette for cheese, and Nicholas for wine. Don't forget to walk into the side streets brimmed with fashion shops, traditional bistros, and trendy bars and restaurants.
Rue Montorgueil, 2nd arr., Metro Sentier

⑧ Somewhat hidden away behind the Pompidou Centre, between Rue du Temple, Rue Rambuteau, and Rue Beaubourg, lies the **Jardin Anne Frank**. This park is the perfect place to escape the hustle and bustle of the city. Look for Anne Frank's chestnut tree—back in 2007, a cutting from the tree Anne described in her diary was planted here by the Anne Frank House in Amsterdam. The garden is also home to the Musée de la Poupée, a doll museum.

14 Impasse Berthaud, 3rd arr., www.paris.fr/equipements/jardin-anne-frank-2737, daily 10am-5:45pm, free, Metro Rambuteau

⑮ Rue des Rosiers is a cozy little street full of Jewish eateries. Parisians love to come here on weekends for falafel. L'As du Falafel is easily recognized by its green facade. Some places are closed on Friday night and Saturday during Sabbath. At number 10, you will find the entrance to a little park where you can eat your falafel on a bench. If you want a sit-down restaurant, try to snag a table at Chez Marianne on the corner of Rue des Hospitalières-Saint-Gervais.

Rue des Rosiers, 4th arr., daily noon-11pm, Metro St.-Paul

Le Village Saint-Paul was established when the neighborhood underwent a period of restoration and renovation. It is a labyrinth of courtyards, galleries, bookshops, antique stores, restaurants, and cafés. Just walking through this secluded, cozy area is a pleasure of its own.

Le Village Saint-Paul, between Quai des Celestins, Rue St.-Paul, and Rue Charlemagne, 4th arr., www.levillagesaintpaul.com, daily 7am-7pm, Metro St.-Paul or Pont Marie

The **Place des Vosges** is thought by many to be the most beautiful square in Paris. The Marais was once a community favored by the aristocracy and wealthy bourgeoisie, and in 1605 King Henry IV had the wonderful idea of making a square park here enclosed by 36 houses. Many famous French people have lived here, including Cardinal Richelieu at number 21 and author Victor Hugo at number 6. This is a good place for a break—either on a bench or on one of the inviting terraces.

Place des Vosges, 4th arr., Metro St.-Paul or Bastille

Le Marché des Enfants Rouges is the oldest market in Paris. It gets its names from an orphanage that used to be nearby and where the children were always dressed in red clothing. The covered market, which is open most days, has about twenty stalls where you can buy a variety of fresh products. The market also has many places to eat, and Parisians from across the city flock here for breakfast, lunch, and dinner.

39 Rue de Bretagne, Tue-Sat 8:30am-7:30pm, Sun 8:30am-2pm, Metro Filles du Calvaire

WALK **4**

LES ÎLES, LATIN QUARTER & SAINT-GERMAIN-DES-PRÉS

ABOUT THE WALK

This route takes you across the Seine to Paris's Left Bank, primarily through the 5th and 6th arrondissements. If you want, split the walk over two days so you have extra time to stop and enjoy the scenic parks you come to along the way. The 5th arrondissement (up to location 23) is especially interesting during the day, and the 6th is great in the early evening when you can relax and enjoy a nice drink and then dinner (locations 24-34).

THE NEIGHBORHOODS

In the heart of the city, smack dab in the middle of the Seine, are the islands **Île de la Cité** and **Île Saint-Louis. Notre-Dame,** which was badly damaged in a fire in April 2019, towers above everything. On the square in front of the cathedral is a bronze compass rose. This is Point Zéro (zero mark), where since 1769 all roads to and from Paris meet. It is no coincidence that this point is located on l'Île de la Cité, the island where Paris originated.

For centuries the Left Bank of the Seine, or Rive Gauche, has had great cultural significance. After the arrival of the university in 1215 and then later a printing press, the Left Bank became the intellectual and literary heart of the city. Scholars, writers, and publishers settled here, along with countless bookshops and writers' cafés. Later, the arrival of artists brought galleries as well. The **Latin Quarter (Quartier Latin)**—Paris's student area—is located around the Sainte-Geneviève hill. **Rue Mouffetard** is one of the oldest streets in Paris, with lots of restaurants and bars.

The **Saint-Germain-des-Prés** neighborhood became an intellectual and literary center. In local nightclubs, philosophy, politics, and literature were discussed against backdrops of smoke and jazz music. Jean-Paul Sartre, Simone de

WALK 4 DESCRIPTION (approx. 7.2 mi/11.6 km)

Start at the Pont Neuf metro station, then cross the bridge to the two buildings on the left in the middle of the bridge. On Rue H. Robert, head to Place
Dauphine ❶. Go left on Quai de l'Horloge until the Boulevard du Palais and turn
right ❷ ❸. You are now on l'Île de la Cité ❹. Cross Pont Saint-Michel and take
an immediate left to the next bridge. Go right on Rue Saint-Jacques for some
Parisian entertainment ❺. Take Quai de Montebello and Pont au Double to the
Notre-Dame area ❻. From here walk around to l'Île Saint-Louis ❼, where you'll
find the best ice cream ❽. Then take Rue des Deux Ponts and cross Pont de
la Tournelle. Go left to the Institut du Monde Arabe ❾. Then walk back to the
Quai de la Tournelle and turn left on Rue de Pontoise. At the end of the street
bear right, then make two lefts to end up at Rue Monge. Take this street, make
a detour into the candy shop ❿ and walk to the arenas ⓫. Walk to the other
side and take Rue des Arènes. Cross Rue Linné to Rue G. de la Brosse, and at
the end of the street turn right to the Jardin des Plantes ⓬, where you can also
visit the zoo ⓭. Exit the garden at Rue Geoffroy-Saint-Hilaire, where there is a
beautiful museum ⓮. Cross the street to La Mosquée de Paris ⓯ and continue on Rue Daubenton. Walk to Rue Mouffetard and take a right ⓰. Keep walking along Rue Mouffetard, to Place de la Contrescarpe ⓱. Take a left on Rue
Thouin to the Panthéon ⓲. Go right to catch a movie ⓳ and visit a museum ⓴
. Walk back a bit and onto Boulevard St.-Michel. Turn left to the park ㉑. Walk
through the park and exit at the Sénat to end up at Rue Férou and continue
to St.-Sulpice. There are great shops ㉒ in Rue du Vieux Colombier. For a nice
gin and tonic bar, take a detour down a side street off Rue St.-Sulpice ㉓. Walk
further for more unique shops ㉔. At the end of Rue St.-Sulpice turn left ㉕ and
cross Boulevard St. Germain to see one of the oldest alleys in the city ㉖. Walk
to the end and take a left on Rue Buci to Rue de Seine ㉗ ㉘ ㉙. Turn right on
Rue de l'Échaude and take Rue Jacob to Rue de Furstemberg, then turn left ㉚.
Continue right on Rue de l'Abbaye to Place St.-Germain-des-Prés and to stop at
a famous café ㉛ and for American food ㉜. Walk down Rue du Dragon to Rue
de Sevres for a nice boutique from a typical French fashion brand ㉝. Walk until
you reach Rue Dupin to end the day ㉞.

SIGHTS & ATTRACTIONS

2 La Conciergerie was Paris's first prison. The revolutionary Georges Danton was one of the many who did time here, along with Marie Antoinette and Robespierre. Marie Antoinette's cell has been made into a commemorative chapel you can visit.

2 Boulevard du Palais, 1st arr., paris-conciergerie.fr, daily 9:30am-6pm, €11.50, Metro Cité

3 The **Sainte-Chapelle** Cathedral was built in the time of Saint Louis of France (Louis IX), to house Christ's crown of thorns and a relic of the Holy Cross. The cathedral has two chapels—a lower chapel for the king's servants and an upper chapel for the royal family. The beautiful stained-glass windows are unique and have significant cultural and historical value.

8 Boulevard du Palais, 1st arr., sainte-chapelle.fr, daily Apr-Sep 9am-7pm, Oct-March 9am-5pm, €11.50, Metro Cité

6 Badly damaged in a fire in April 2019, **Notre-Dame de Paris** stands on Île de la Cité and, despite its closure as it undergoes repairs, still draws many visitors. Services are held in other churches in the city. The renovation of the cathedral is expected to last more than five years. Check the Notre-Dame website for the calendar and the latest news on the renovation.

6 Parvis Notre-Dame, 4th arr., www.notredamedeparis.fr, not open to the public, Metro Cité or St.-Michel

9 The building that houses the **Institut du Monde Arabe** was designed in the 1980s by Jean Nouvel. Outside, it is covered in thousands of small steel mobile apertures, which gradually open and close based on the amount of sunshine. Inside you'll find an impressive collection of Arabic design, including contemporary art, calligraphy, and musical instruments. Head up to the rooftop terrace and enjoy the view over the Seine and Notre-Dame.

1 Rue des Fossés Saint-Bernard, 5th arr., www.imarabe.org, Tue-Fri 10am-6pm, Sat-Sun 10am-7pm, €8, Metro Jussieu

⑪ A Roman amphitheater from the 1st century, the **Arènes de Lutèce** is probably the oldest remaining building in Paris. In Roman times theater plays and gladiator fights were held here. Seating in the amphitheater was able to accommodate approximately 17,000 spectators. After the fall of the Roman Empire, the location of the theater was unknown for a long time. At the start of the twentieth century the theater was found, excavated, partly renovated, and opened as a public square.
47 Rue Monge, 5th arr., en.parisinfo.com/paris-museum-monument/71451/arenes-de- lutece-et-square-capitan, daily March 8am-7pm, April & Sep 8am-8:30pm, May-Aug 8am-9:30pm, Oct-Feb 8am-5:45pm, free, Metro Cardinal Lemoine

⑭ In **Muséum National d'Histoire Naturelle's** Grande Galerie de l'Évolution you can learn all about evolution and the relationship between nature and humans. This beautifully renovated glass-and-metal space contains an unprecedented collection of taxidermied animals.
36 Rue Geoffroy-Saint-Hilaire, 5th arr., www.mnhn.fr, Mon & Wed-Sun 10am-6pm, €10, Metro Austerlitz or Jussieu

⑱ The **Panthéon** is one of the greatest works of architect Soufflot. This neoclassical dome with pillars makes a stately impression. Following the French Revolution, this former church was transformed into a crypt where countless famous French figures are interred. More than 70 notable men of stature have been laid to rest here, including Voltaire, Rousseau, Hugo, and Zola. Recently, dancer and resistance heroine Josephine Baker was interred in the Panthéon.
Place du Panthéon, 5th arr., www.paris-pantheon.fr, daily April-Sept 10am-6:30pm, Oct-March 10am-6pm, €11.50, Metro Cardinal Lemoine

⑳ **Musée de Cluny** is dedicated to the Middle Ages. Many stories from this time are reflected in the series of tapestries entitled *The Lady and the Unicorn*—a perfect example of the millefleurs style. Don't forget to check out the Gallo-Roman baths too.
28 Rue du Sommerard, 5th arr., www.musee-moyenage.fr, Mon & Wed-Sun 9:15am-5:45pm, €5, Metro Odéon

㉚ **Musée National Eugène Delacroix** is located in the house where the painter previously lived. The artist's former studio paints a good picture not only of Delacroix himself, but also of the artistic movement he was a part of: Romanticism. Be sure to also walk back to the beautiful hidden square Place de Furstenberg.

6 Rue de Furstemberg, 6th arr., www.musee-delacroix.fr, Mon & Wed-Sun 9:30am-11:30am & 1pm-5:30pm, €7, Metro St.-Germain-des-Prés or Mabillon

FOOD & DRINK

❺ **Aux Trois Mailletz**—you either love it or you hate it. This isn't a place you go for an outstanding meal but rather for the atmosphere and entertainment. Enjoy a drink and piano music upstairs, or head into the basement for music, dance, and a show. Among Parisians, Trois Mailletz has long since been known as a place to go for a fun—albeit always unpredictable—evening.

56 Rue Galande, 5th arr., auxtroismailletz.com, tel. 01 43540079, daily 7pm-4am, €25, Metro Cité or St.-Michel Notre-Dame

❼ The **Saint-Régis** is a typical Parisian café and the perfect place for a glass of wine with some cheese or a good lunch. It is located on the most beautiful square of Île Saint-Louis. And via the bridge you walk straight into the gardens of Notre-Dame.

6 Rue Jean du Bellay, 4th arr., www.lesaintregis-paris.com, tel. 01 43545941, daily 7am-2am, € 10, Metro Pont Marie

❽ Ice cream in France isn't nearly as popular as gelato in Italy. However, **Berthillon** is an exception to the rule. This shop has irresistibly delicious sorbets and is hands down the best ice cream in Paris. You'll want to stand in line for that!

31 Rue Saint-Louis on Île Saint-Louis, 4th arr., www.berthillon.fr, tel. 01 43543161, Wed-Sun 10am-8pm, Metro Pont Marie

17 Ernest Hemingway once described **Café Delmas**'s predecessor—Café des Amateurs—as "the cesspool of the Rue Mouffetard." The current Café Delmas is enormously popular among local high school students. The terrace is nice and spacious and is the perfect place to soak up the neighborhood vibe.

2 Place de la Contrescarpe, 5th arr., cafedelmas.com, tel. 01 43265126, daily 9am-1:30am, €18, Metro Cardinal Lemoine

23 Of all the bars around Odéon, **Tiger** is the best looking. The floors are tiled with blue mosaic, the walls are covered with a green jungle print, and the three different areas of the bar—laid out on different levels—are separated by wooden structures. At Tiger, everything revolves around gin, and the charming bartenders mix drinks with one hundred varieties of it. So if gin and tonic is your thing, then this is the place for you—Tiger serves some 1,040 combinations.

13 Rue Princesse, 6th arr., www.tiger-paris.com, tel. 01 84058174, daily 5:30pm-2am, from €11, Metro Mabillon

㉕ **The Cod House** is a Japanese tapas and cocktail bar. On the menu are dishes like sashimi, bento, and California sushi rolls. And there are other surprises such as patatas bravas Tokyo-style. This is a great place for a cocktail and some small dishes to snack on. It's spacious and light with comfortable sofas.

1 Rue de Condé, 6th arr., www.thecodhouse.fr, tel. 01 42493559, Mon 7:30pm-2am, Tue-Sat noon-3pm & 7:30pm-2am, Sun noon-3pm, sushi roll €12, Metro Odéon

㉗ **Huguette** on Rue de Seine feels like a stretch of beach right in the middle of Saint-Germain-des-Prés. With a plate of oysters and a bottle of white wine, the hip, sunny terrace is a great place to while away the time. Huguette is technically a bistro de la mer (seafood bistro), but there are also a few meat dishes on the menu. Inside the restaurant to the right is a cute market-style corner area where fish is prepared, and you can even get it to go.

81 Rue de Seine, 6th arr., www.huguette-bistro.com, tel. 01 43250028, daily noon-11:30pm, €21, Metro Mabillon

㉘ The terrace at **Bar du Marché** is an ideal spot for people watching. The café is on the corner of Rue de Buci—a nice, busy market street. The friendly servers, with their blue overalls and newsboy caps, will remind you of street kids from a forgotten era.

75 Rue de Seine, 6th arr., tel. 01 43265515, Mon & Fri 7:30am-2am, Tue-Thu & Sat-Sun 8am-2am, €15, Metro Mabillon or Odéon

㉙ Whether you sit inside or outside, **La Palette** is a great spot. Inside, the café's Art Deco style is reminiscent of 20th century Paris. Outside, the green and sunny terrace is a nice place to relax. Stop by and order a traditional apéro: an aperitif with a cheese platter or some sausage.

43 Rue de Seine, 6th arr., www.lapalette-paris.com, tel. 01 46348411, Mon-Sat 8am-2am, Sun 10am-2am, €22, Metro Mabillon

㉛ You can't say you've truly experienced Saint-Germain-des-Prés until you've had a coffee at **Café de Flore.** You can almost taste the café's history. Existentialists such as Jean-Paul Sartre and Simone de Beauvoir were regulars here, as were Pablo Picasso and writer André Breton.

172 Boulevard Saint-Germain, 6th arr., www.cafedeflore.fr, tel. 01 45485526, daily 7:30am-1:30am, lunch €18, Metro St.-Germain des Prés

32 Tucked away in the courtyard of an old hotel is **Ralph's,** the luxurious restaurant of fashion designer Ralph Lauren. The menu offers typical American fare, such as steak, burgers, and Caesar salad, but it's a touch more upscale. For example, you can order a cheeseburger with a glass of champagne. Ralph's is not inexpensive, but it does stand out when you're looking for fine American food in Paris.

173 Boulevard Saint-Germain, 6th arr., www.ralphlauren.fr/en/global/ralphs-paris/7120, tel. 01 44777600, daily in summer noon-5pm & 7pm-11pm, winter noon-5pm & 7pm-10:30pm, €35, Metro St.-Germain des Prés

34 In this French bistro you'll find locals and tourists alike. **L'Epi Dupin** is a nice place to go with friends to enjoy a good meal. The food is beautifully presented, and the menu changes regularly. Considering the quality, the prices are also quite reasonable. This restaurant is popular, so it's best to reserve a table in advance.

11 Rue Dupin, 6th arr., www.epidupin.com, tel. 01 42226456, Tue-Sat noon-3pm & 7pm-10:30pm, €28, Metro Sèvres Babylone

SHOPPING

10 **Le Bonbon au Palais** (The Candy Palace) is a wonderful shop, with glass candy dishes full of sweets from across France. The enthusiastic owner will happily tell you about each candy, including where it comes from and what makes it so special. Who knows, he might even let you sample something, such as the candied violets made with all-natural ingredients.

19 Rue Monge, 5th arr., lebonbonaupalais.com, Tue-Sat 10:30am-7pm, Metro Cardinal Lemoine

22 Within the French world of fashion, **Agnès B.** is something of a household name. Pieces from the brand's comfortable and stylish collection are the basics

in any Parisian fashionista's wardrobe—be it woman or man. The Agnès b
femme and homme lines are presented in a decor that perfectly complements
the clothing.

6 Rue du Vieux Colombier, 6th arr., www.agnesb.fr, Mon-Sat 11am-7pm, Metro St.-
Sulpice

㉔ Trudon is a family business that has been around since 1643. They make
candles and home perfumes. The candles are handmade in Normandy and
smell wonderful. During the time of Louis the XIV, Trudon was the court supplier
for Versailles.

78 Rue de Seine, 6th Arr., www.trudon.com, Mon 11am-7pm, Tues-Sat 10:30am-
7:30pm, Metro Mabillon

㉝ Wondering where all those Parisiennes buy their stylish outfits? Chances are
at **Maje.** This French fashion brand is Paris incarnated, and it is dearly loved by
the locals. Expect feminine items of high quality.

15 Rue de Sèvres, 6th arr., us.maje.com, Mon-Sat 10:30am-7:30pm, Sun 11am-7pm,
Metro Sèvre Babylone

MORE TO EXPLORE

❶ This square, located behind the Palais de Justice, is a pleasant and unexpected place to sit and take a break. The stately buildings surrounding **Place
Dauphine** block out the noise of the city, and in the summer, the trees provide
full shade. There are plenty of benches where you can relax and read a book or
observe a game of Pétanque.

Place Dauphine, l'Île de la Cité, 1st arr., Metro Pont Neuf

❹ L'Île de la Cité is the island around which Paris developed. It was originally two
uninhabited islands, Île aux Vaches ("island of cows") and Île Notre-Dame, which
belonged to the cathedral. In the early 17th century, the two islands were joined
by Christophe Marie, and by around 1664 they were completely built up. The island is connected to the rest of Paris on both the left and right banks. It's a nice
place for a walk, or you can just sit on one of the terraces along the waterfront.

4th arr., Metro Cité

⑫ The beautiful **Jardin des Plantes** is a must-see for all garden lovers. You can walk through the botanic gardens and the rose gardens and visit the giant greenhouses. There is even a zoo and a playground here.

57 Rue Cuvier, 5th arr., www.jardindesplantesdeparis.fr, gardens open daily, 8am-5:30pm, greenhouses open Mon & Wed-Sun 10am-5pm, garden free, greenhouses €7, Metro Gare d'Austerlitz

⑬ In the middle of the city, hidden in the park, you will find **Ménagerie du Jardin des Plantes.** This zoo is home to more than 200 animal species, of which a third is threatened with extinction and part of a breeding program. It's the perfect getaway to escape the city buzz, especially with children.

57, Rue Cuvier, 5th arr., www.zoodujardindesplantes.fr, daily 10am-5pm, €13, Metro Gare d'Austerlitz

⑮ **La Mosquée de Paris** was built in 1922 as a monument to Muslim victims of the First World War. The mosque is open to the public, but don't forget to take your shoes off when you enter. Here you can treat your body and soul at the hammam and in the prayer hall. There is also an excellent tearoom where you can enjoy mint tea and a large assortment of sweets and other yummy snacks. For a full meal, try the restaurant.

39 Rue Saint-Hilaire, 5th arr., www.mosqueedeparis.net, Mon-Thur & Sat-Sun 9am-6pm, restaurant 11:30am-midnight, tearoom open 9am-midnight, hammam 10am-9pm, €3, Metro Place Monge

⑯ One of Paris's oldest streets, **Rue Mouffetard** dates back to the time of Roman domination. During the Middle Ages, many craftsmen had their shops here because of the proximity to the Bièvre River. Be sure to pay attention to all the ornamentation on the building facades, such as the painting at number 134. The famous morning market nearby at Église Saint-Médard has been around since the seventh century. Local producers sell their products here—from fresh fruits and vegetables to homemade cheeses. The many restaurants and cafés along the street also make a stroll here well worth your while.

Rue Mouffetard, 5th arr., market open Wed, Fri & Sun 8am-2pm, Metro Place Monge

🔞 **Cinéma du Panthéon** is one of the oldest movie theaters in Paris. Come here not just to catch a movie, but also for a drink or bite to eat at Le Salon, which was decorated by none other than Catherine Deneuve. Note: Le Salon is open only during the week.

13 Rue Victor Cousin, 5th arr., www.whynotproductions.fr, movie theater: see website for times and prices, salon: Mon-Fri noon-7pm, Metro Luxembourg or Cluny-la Sorbonne

⭐ **Luxembourg Gardens** is a wonderful park where Parisians love to come to relax, have fun, and walk around. The park is dotted throughout with the iconic "Luxembourg chairs." Also located here is the Palais de Luxembourg, which was built between 1615 and 1627 for Marie de Médici and today houses the French Senate.

Rue de Vaurigard/Boulevard Saint-Michel, 6th arr., www.senat.fr/visite/jardin, from sunrise to sunset, free, Metro Luxembourg or Odéon

㉖ **La Cour du Commerce Saint-André** is a 400-foot-long (122-meters-long) passageway. It dates to 1776 and is one of the few streets in Paris untouched by the large-scale restructuring of the city by Baron Haussmann at the behest of Napoleon III. Here you'll find the oldest restaurant in Paris, Le Procope, which opened back in 1686. Queen Marie Antoinette and Emperor Napoleon ate here in their time. Treading on the original cobblestones of La Cour du Commerce Saint-André feels a bit like stepping back in time to medieval Paris.

La Cour du Commerce St.-André, 6th arr., free, Metro Odéon

WALK **5**

EIFFEL TOWER, INVALIDES & CHAMPS-ÉLYSÉES

ABOUT THE WALK

This long walk is best to do when the weather is nice. You can follow this route forward or backward. The section of the route from the Eiffel Tower over Les Berges de la Seine and up to Rue de Bac can be done by bike as well. You can also cycle the Champs-Élysées from the Concorde to the Arc de Triomphe—it's a decent stretch—but be sure to get off your bike before the Arc de Triomphe roundabout. If you'd rather not walk the Champs-Élysées, hop on Metro line 1.

THE NEIGHBORHOODS

Paris is full of grand, historical buildings. The city can thank Louis XIV for its classic character and Renaissance influence. In the 17th century, he had **Les Invalides** built; it's where his wounded officers and soldiers were taken for care. Later Napoleon introduced the Empire style in Paris, which had ancient Egyptian and Roman influences. And he had the **Arc de Triomphe** built. Between 1852 and 1870, during the Second French Empire under the rule of Napoleon III, Paris's classic, wide boulevards and avenues were built.

Avenue des Champs-Élysées connects the Place Charles de Gaulle, where the Arc de Triomphe stands, with the **Place de la Concorde.** It dates to the 17th century—a time when it was a long road in a part of the city with little going on. In 1828, the first sidewalks were constructed. Today, the **Champs-Élysées** is renowned the world over as a shopping mecca. All the best-known retail chains are represented here, and the shops are open long hours. There are also several big movie theaters on this boulevard.

In the late 19th century, French architects began to incorporate materials such as iron and glass into their work. This new style is reflected in the **Eiffel Tower,**

WALK 5 DESCRIPTION (approx. 7.75 mi/12.5 km)

Start this walk in the late morning to make sure the museums you pass along the way are already open. From the Iéna metro station, walk toward the Palais de Tokyo ① ② and reserve a table for the evening at a fancy restaurant ③. Head right on Rue de la Manutention to Avenue New York. Head right toward Place du Trocadéro, where the Palais de Chaillot is located ④. Peek inside for a great view of the Eiffel Tower. Then walk down the stairs and across the bridge to the Eiffel Tower ⑤. Stop and take in a museum on the Quai Branly ⑥ ⑦. If you take the stairs down to the Seine, you'll reach a new path for pedestrians and cyclists, which used to be part of the road ⑧. Turn right on Avenue Bosquet and take the third left on Rue Saint-Dominque for a nice neighborhood café ⑨ or typical French shops ⑩. Here you will also find a nice brasserie ⑪. Go left on Boulevard de la Tour Maubourg. Walk to the Seine and go right. Keep walking until you reach Pont Alexandre III ⑫. Here you can get something to drink ⑬ or enjoy tapas on a boat ⑭. Take the stairs back up and walk down Avenue du Marechal Gallieni to Les Invalides ⑮. In front of the building turn left, then right on Boulevard des Invalides. Take the first street to the left. After the Musée Rodin ⑯, take the first street to the right, Rue Barbet de Jouy. Follow this to the end to Rue de Babylone and turn left for lunch or coffee ⑰. Continue until Rue du Bac. To the right is a high-end department store ⑱. Walk back to Rue du Bac to check out the Conran Shop ⑲ or a beauty concept store ⑳. Turn left on Rue de Varenne, take the first right, Rue de Bellechasse, and immediately another right onto Rue de Grenelle. Walk past the Dutch ambassador's residence ㉑ until you reach Boulevard Raspail. Walk a few feet to the left, cross over, and walk down Rue de Luynes for a nice coffee shop ㉒. Turn left on Boulevard Saint-Germain and turn right at Rue du Bac. Stop at Deyrolle and take in all the beautiful things there ㉓. Further ahead, turn left on Rue de Lille toward the Musée d'Orsay ㉔. Cross the Seine via the Passerelle Léopold-Sédar-Senghor. Walk through the Jardin des Tuileries to the Place de la Concorde ㉕ ㉖ ㉗. Go left from here ㉘ ㉙ and walk up the Champs-Élysées ㉚ ㉛. Wrap up the day in style ㉜ ㉝. At the end of the Champs-Élysées is the Arc de Triomphe ㉞.

SIGHTS & ATTRACTIONS

1 The exhibitions in the experimental 21st-century exhibit space **Palais de Tokyo** are always unique and boundary-pushing, with light and sound effects and moving objects. The space is enormous, so it can contain large objects. The exhibits vary tremendously, but there is always something to discover. The museum shop is also worth a visit—it sells unique books and fun knickknacks. The restaurant with a terrace serves international fare.

13 Avenue du Président Wilson, 16th arr., www.palaisdetokyo.com, Mon & Wed-Sun noon-midnight, €12, Metro Iéna

2 The **Musée d'Art Moderne** is in the same building as the Palais de Tokyo. The building was constructed for the 1937 World's Fair. In this museum of modern art, you'll find an extensive collection of 20th- and 21st-century art owned by the city of Paris.

11 Avenue du Président Wilson, 16th arr., www.mam.paris.fr, Tues-Wed & Fri-Sun 10am-6pm, Thurs 10am-10pm, free to permanent collection, Metro Iéna or Alma-Marceau

4 The neoclassical **Palais de Chaillot**, designed by four architects, was built for the 1937 World's Fair. Today it houses the museum La Cité de l'Architecture et du Patrimoine. Even if you're not interested in visiting the museum, take a look inside. Out back is a terrace with an amazing view of the Eiffel Tower.

1 Place du Trocadéro, 16th arr., www.citechaillot.fr, Mon, Wed & Fri-Sun 11am-7pm, Thurs 11am-9pm, €9, Metro Trocadéro

5 The **Eiffel Tower** was built for the 1889 World's Fair. Initially Gustave Eiffel's design was met with great resistance, but the Eiffel Tower has since become the symbol of Paris. From the third balcony you can see as far as 40 miles (65 km) away. The line to visit the tower is often never-ending—sometimes it helps to go either very early or very late. Tip: buy your ticket online beforehand.

Champ de Mars, 7th arr., www.toureiffel.paris, daily 9:30am-10:45pm, €10.50-€26.10, Metro Bir-Hakeim

⑥ The **Musée du Quai Branly**, which opened in 2006, is in a striking building. This museum of les arts lointains exhibits approximately 3,500 works of indigenous art from Africa and Oceania among other places. The building is surrounded by a beautiful park with a mur végétal (wall of plants) on the Seine side.
37 Quai Branly, 7th arr., www.quaibranly.fr, Tue-Wed & Sat-Sun 10:30am-7pm, Thu 10:30am-10pm, €12, Metro Iéna or Alma-Marceau

⑫ **Pont Alexandre III** is the most elegant bridge in Paris, not least of all because of its beautiful golden statues. It was built over two years and was opened for the 1900 World's Fair.
Pont Alexandre III, 8th arr., Metro Champs-Élysées Clemenceau or Invalides

⑮ In 1670 Louis XIV had **Les Invalides** built as a resting place for soldiers wounded during his numerous wars. In 1861, Napoleon was laid to rest here in the crypt under the golden dome. The building also houses the Musée de l'Armée, which is dedicated to the history of the army. Whenever a new French president is inaugurated, the cannons in front of Les Invalides fire 21 times.
129 Rue de Grenelle, 7th arr., www.musee-armee.fr, Mon & Wed-Sun 10am-6pm, Tue 10am-9pm, €14, courtyard free, Metro Invalides

⑯ **Musée Rodin** is in the former residence of the sculptor. In addition to Rodin's own sculptures and studies, the museum also exhibits the work of Camille Claudel, Rodin's mistress and model. In the garden there are several famous statues, including *Le Penseur* (*The Thinker*). The charming museum and the beautiful garden can be visited separately.
77 Rue de Varenne, 7th arr., www.musee-rodin.fr, Tue-Sun 10am-6:30pm, €13, Metro Varenne or Invalides

㉑ Since 1920 **Hôtel d'Avaray,** recognizable by the lions above the enormous door, has been the official residence of the Dutch ambassador to France. This house has been the set of numerous films, including *The Intouchables*, *Les Saveurs du Palais*, and *Le Capital*. The gorgeous residence is exclusively for professional use and is therefore not open to the public.
85 Rue de Grenelle, 7th arr., not open to the public, Metro Rue du Bac

24 **Musée d'Orsay** is housed in a 19th-century train station that was renovated in 1986 and made into a museum. In the grand hall, the station's enormous clock still hangs. Sculptures line the wide balconies, and in the exhibit halls you'll find a collection of Impressionist paintings. In addition to the museum café, the museum also has two great restaurants worth trying, which are open only to museum visitors.

1 Rue de la Légion d'Honneur, 7th arr., www.musee-orsay.fr, Tue-Wed & Fri-Sun 9:30am-6pm, Thu 9:30am-9:45pm, €16, courtyard free, Metros Solférino, Assemblée Nationale, Concorde, or Tuileries

25 **Jeu de Paume** got its name from the fact that in 1851 Napoleon III played tennis in the hall of the building. For the past few years, this building has housed the Centre National de la Photographie, where you can see modern photography exhibits.

1 Place de la Concorde, 8th arr., www.jeudepaume.org, Tue 11am-9pm, Wed-Sun 11am-7pm, €10, Metro Concorde

26 **Musée de l'Orangerie** was once a greenhouse where oranges were grown. The main attraction here is Claude Monet's famous painting *Les Nymphéas* (*Water Lilies*). You can also check out the Walter-Guillaume collection, with works from 20th-century painters.

Jardin Tuileries, 1st arr., www.musee-orangerie.fr, tel. 01 44778007, Mon & Wed-Sun 9am-6pm, €12.50, Metro Concorde

27 **Place de la Concorde,** the biggest square in Paris, was the backdrop of bloody scenes during the French Revolution, because it was here that the guillotine stood. It was following this tense time that the square received its current name, which refers to harmony. In the middle stands the 3,000-year-old Luxor obelisk, gifted to the French king Louis-Philippe in 1831 by the Egyptian viceroy Muhammad Ali.

Place de la Concorde, 1st arr., Metro Concorde

28 **Le Petit Palais** houses the Musée des Beaux-Arts de la Ville de Paris. There is a large collection of art here, including works from artists Ingres, Delacroix, and Courbet, among others. The café in the courtyard is a secret oasis.

Avenue Winston Churchill, 8th arr., www.petitpalais.paris.fr, Tues-Sun 10am-6pm, free to the permanent collection, Metro Champs-Élysées Clemenceau or Concorde

29 **Le Grand Palais** was built for the 1900 World's Fair, together with Le Petit Palais and the Pont Alexandre III. It is made of concrete, steel, and glass. The enormous glass ceiling is particularly impressive. Inside the building you'll find, among other things, temporary exhibitions (Galeries Nationales du Grand Palais) and a science museum (Palais de la Découverte).

3 Avenue du Général Eisenhower, 8th arr., www.grandpalais.fr, see website for opening hours and prices, Metro Champs-Élysées Clémenceau or Franklin Roosevelt

34 In 1806, one year after the victory at Austerlitz, Napoleon commissioned the building of the **Arc de Triomphe**. It wasn't until 1836, however, that the arch of triumph was completed. The four large reliefs on the pillars' pedestal commemorate the victory of 1805. In 1921, the Tomb of the Unknown Soldier was interred under the arches. This made the Arc de Triomphe a memorial to the First World War. From the top, you can look out over the Champs-Élysées. Opening hours are dependent on the weather.

Place Charles de Gaulle, 8th arr., www.paris-arc-de-triomphe.fr, daily 10am-10:30pm, €13, Metro Charles de Gaulle-Étoile

FOOD & DRINK

3 Find a seat on the ground floor or on the terrace and enjoy the gorgeous view out over the Seine and the Eiffel Tower. The inside of **Monsieur Bleu** is modern, elegant, and calm, and for Paris the tables are quite spaciously placed. This is a trendy place, with DJs to create a nice atmosphere for dinner. The Eastern-style tuna steak is highly recommended.

20 Avenue de New York, 16th arr., monsieurbleu.com, tel. 01 47209047, daily noon-2am, €35, Metro Iéna or Alma-Marceau

❼ On the rooftop of the Musée de Branly you'll find the fine dining restaurant **Les Ombres,** known for its romantic view of the Eiffel Tower. Expect delicious, refined food in small portions.

27 Quai Branly, 7th arr., www.lesombres-restaurant.com, tel. 01 47536800, Tue-Sun 7pm-10:30, €40, Metro Alma Marceau

❾ Neighborhood café **Le Malabar** is beloved by locals, and it's not hard to see why: fresh cocktails, delicious comfort food, attentive service, and a good atmosphere. The menu is modern French, ideal for a casual lunch or dinner.

88 Rue Saint Dominique, 7th arr., www.lemalabarparis.com, tel. 01 45513144, daily 8am-2am, €10, Metro La Tour-Maubourg

⓫ Ever since the roaring twenties **Brasserie Thoumieux** has been one of the most popular restaurants on the Left Bank of Paris. The allure of that Art Deco period has been preserved in the interior, but with a modern twist. The menu is classically French with delicious escargots, confit de canard, and an éclair with caramel to go. Yum! Try the Sunday brunch. Every Thursday, Friday, and Saturday night there is live piano music.

79 Rue Saint Dominique, 7th arr., tel. 01 47057900, brasseriethoumieux.fr, daily noon-2:30pm & 7pm-11pm, €30, Metro 8 to La Tour-Maubourg

⓭ **Faust** is located under the Pont Alexandre III and offers three options: a terrace for something to drink, an elegant restaurant, and a club. If you keep walking under the bridge, you'll find many more terraces. This is a particularly hopping place on Friday nights during the summer months.

Pont Alexandre III, 7th arr., www.faustparis.fr, tel. 01 44186060, daily noon-2am, club is open Fri-Sat 11:30pm-7am, set lunch €26, Metro Champs-Élysées Clemenceau or Invalides

⓮ Following the success of Rosa Bonheur in Parc Buttes Chaumont, **Rosa Bonheur sur Seine** is the second installment of this popular nighttime location. The boat, constructed of wood and glass, features both a restaurant and a nightclub. Enjoy a stone-fired pizza, while watching the boats go by on the river

Seine. Then at night, the space transforms into a dance club, which also hosts concerts and other events.
Quai d'Orsay, Port des Invalides, 7th arr., www.rosabonheur.fr, tel. 01 47536692, Wed-Fri 6pm-1:30am, Sat noon-1:30am, Sun noon-11pm, €15, Metro Invalides

17 Coutume Café is the place to go in this embassy area for a special coffee, lunch, or weekend brunch. Coffee aficionados come here to buy exotic beans. On Saturday and Sunday, you can choose from three types of brunch: classic, detox veggie, or Sumatran. Whichever you opt for, you're sure to leave with a full belly.
47 Rue de Babylone 7th arr., www.coutumecafe.com, tel. 01 45515047, Mon-Fri 8:30am-5:30pm, Sat-Sun 9am-6pm, lunch €17, Metro St.-Francois Xavier

22 Fancy a cup of coffee? Go to **Noir.** This trendy coffee bar serves delicious coffee made with locally roasted beans. The baristas are not only professionally trained but also very friendly. If you're a true lover of coffee, you can order beans on their website.
9 Rue de Luynes, 7th arr., www.noircoffeeshop.com, tel. 07 80982197, daily 8am-6pm, espresso €2.50, Metro Rue du Bac

32 The restaurant **Le Drugstore** is an ideal spot for a business lunch, and the service is set up to accommodate this. Come here for quick, friendly service and excellent food. It's located in the Publicis building, one of France's best-known businesses. Its concept was inspired by places in New York. In addition to the restaurant, there is also a pharmacy open 24 hours a day, a bookstore, and a small grocery store.
133 Avenue des Champs-Élysées, 8th arr., www.publicisdrugstore.com, tel. 01 44437764, Mon-Fri 8am-2am, Sat-Sun 10am-2am, €26, Metro Charles de Gaulle-Étoile

33 When you have something to celebrate, **Le Chiberta** is the perfect place. Guy Savoy's stylish restaurant has a Michelin star. Here you can enjoy classic, refined French cuisine. Choose from dishes such as oysters, pigeon en croûte, or red mullet with seaweed butter. The wine list is outstanding—and the bottles are even incorporated into the décor.

3 Rue Arsène Houssaye, 8th arr., www.lechiberta.com, tel. 01 53534200, Mon-Fri noon-2:30pm & 7:30pm-11pm, Sat noon-2:30pm & 7pm-11:30pm, tasting menu €120, Metro Charles de Gaulle-Étoile

SHOPPING

⑩ Rue Saint Dominique is the most fun shopping street in the 7th arrondissement, and you shouldn't skip **Ba&sh.** Designers of this brand are Barbara and Sharon, two stylish Parisians and best friends. Together they design romantic and feminine clothing of top quality—with that typical French je ne sais quoi style.

81 Rue Saint Dominique, 7th arr., www.ba-sh.com, Mon-Sat 10:30am-7:30pm, Metro La Tour-Maubourg

⑱ The luxury department store **Le Bon Marché Rive Gauche** is mostly visited by Parisians. You can find all the high-end brands here. During the week, it's nice to take your time and enjoy looking around. There is a second Le Bon Marché store at number 38, La Grande Épicerie de Paris, which is all about gourmet food—an absolute must see for any and every foodie.

24 Rue de Sèvres, 7th arr., www.lebonmarche.com, Mon-Sat 10am-7:45pm, Sun 11am-7:45pm, Metro Sèvres Babylone

⑲ The concept for this enormous store full of design items, gadgets, and things for the home was imported from London. At the popular **Conran Shop** you'll find the perfect mix of design classics and new items by young designers. Always a good place to stop in and look around.

117 Rue du Bac, 7th arr., www.conranshop.fr, Mon-Fri 10am-7:30pm, Sat 10am-8pm, Sun 11am-7pm, Metro Sèvres Babylone

⑳ Oh My Cream! is a beauty concept store. It sells skincare and makeup, all free of harmful chemicals or with organic ingredients. Discover new brands and get advice on the latest beauty trends. Fans aren't just Parisians.

104 Rue du Bac, 7th arr., www.ohmycream.com, Mon 2pm-7pm, Tue-Sat 10:30am-7:30pm, Metro Sèvres Babylone

㉓ Deyrolle is an experience in its own. Creaking floors, old cases full of rarities, butterflies, seashells, and taxidermied animals everywhere—there's so much to see. Above all, for more than 100 years this store has been making beautiful educational materials, which you'll find plenty of here.
46 Rue du Bac, 7th arr., www.deyrolle.com, Tues-Sat 10am-7pm,
Metro Rue du Bac

㉛ Louis Ernest Ladurée opened **Ladurée** in 1862. It is a chic bakery and tea salon, and little inside has changed since the store first opened. The choice of delectables here is endless, though you must try the famous macarons they are known for. Tip: the restaurant is a good place for breakfast.
75 Avenue des Champs-Élysées, 8th arr., www.laduree.com, shop is open daily 8am-9:30pm, restaurant is open daily 8am-10:30pm, macarons start at €1.50, Metro George V

MORE TO EXPLORE

❽ The city of Paris recently closed **Les Berges de la Seine** to cars and opened it for recreation. Now Parisians can stroll, walk, bike, skate, and run to their hearts' content along this street. In summer, especially, there are many activities organized here. This is an ideal spot for taking a nice walk along the Seine.
Between Pont de l'Alma and the Louvre along the Seine, lesberges.paris.fr, free, Metro Alma-Marceau or Invalides

㉚ The **Champs-Élysées,** la plus belle avenue du monde (the most beautiful avenue in the world), is a street where today you can shop endlessly in stores that also have locations elsewhere. The side streets Avenue Montaigne and Avenue George V are home to the flagship stores of brands such as Dior, Chanel, and all other major French fashion names.
Champs-Élysées, 8th arr., Metros Franklin D Roosevelt, George V, or Champs-Élysées Clemenceau

WALK **6**

BELLEVILLE, CANAL SAINT-MARTIN & MÉNILMONTANT

ABOUT THE WALK

This walk takes you through working-class neighborhoods and artsy areas. Along the way you can stop for lunch, hang out in a park, or mingle among the locals for a picnic by the water. The Bassin de la Villette and Canal Saint-Martin are especially fun in the afternoon. You can easily do this walk either forward or backward. There are very few famous sights or attractions along the route aside from the Père-Lachaise cemetery, which you can also go to directly by metro.

THE NEIGHBORHOODS

The working-class neighborhoods Belleville, Canal Saint-Martin, and Ménilmontant are in the 10th and 19th arrondissements on the Right Bank. In recent years, many more hip spots have been popping up near the **Canal Saint-Martin** and **Bassin de la Villette,** from secondhand shops and hotels to great restaurants and cultural hot spots. Just relaxing along the water—walking, biking, and picnicking—in and of itself is a good time.

The landscaping in **Parc des Buttes-Chaumont** is one of a kind. From the highest point of the buttes (hills) you can look out over Sacré-Coeur and the blue-collar **Belleville** neighborhood where singer Édith Piaf grew up. You can still get a taste of the Paris of yesteryear in this neighborhood.

In the middle of Belleville is a small, little-known park called **Parc de Belleville.** Walking up the hill in this park is exponentially better than spending hours in line for the Eiffel Tower: the view is amazing.

Small streets near the park are full of unique shops, including pop-up stores where young designers sell their products. One thing to note about the area is that it doesn't really come to life until after lunch.

WALK 6 DESCRIPTION (approx. 8.9 mi/14 km)

From the Jaurès metro station, walk to Bassin de la Villette ❶ ❷. Play a game of Pétanque along the way ❸, then go for a beer further down ❹. Walk back and turn left on Rue E. Dehaynin to the park ❺. Head to the exit on Rue de la Villette for some shopping ❻. The street turns into Rue Jean-Baptiste Dumay. Turn left on Rue des Pyrénées, then right at Villa de l'Ermitage ❼. If you're not interested in going to Père-Lachaise, turn right on Rue de Ménilmonant and right on Rue de la Mare to continue with the walk. Otherwise continue on Rue Boyer ❽, Rue de la Bidassoa and Rue des Rondeux to Père-Lachaise ❾. Exit at Boulevard de Ménilmontant. Turn right into the Passage Monplaisir, then take Rue des Panoyaux and Rue Delaitre to the Église Notre-Dame de la Croix. After the church head left on Rue de la Mare, take another left on Rue Henri Chevreau, then turn right on Rue des Couronnes and walk through Passage Plantin to the park ❿ ⓫ for a great view. Head back down via Rue des Couronnes and visit local artists ⓬. Take Rue Francis Picabia to Rue Ramponeau and turn right. Turn left on Rue Jouye-Rouve ⓭. Continue on Rue Rébéval ⓮. Walk all the way to Boulevard de la Villette, cross the street, and turn right. Walk a short stretch on Rue de Sambre-et-Meuse and turn left on Rue St.-Marthe for a cozy little square ⓯. Turn left on Avenue Claude Vellefaux, then right on Rue Alibert ⓰ to the Canal St.-Martin ⓱. Make an immediate right on Quai de Jemappes for an extraordinary cultural center ⓲. Walk along the canal, cross the bridge, and turn right ⓳. Walk straight on Rue des Récollets ⓴ or feast your eyes just past the bridge ㉑ ㉒ ㉓. Otherwise, go left after the bridge on Quai de Valmy. Walk and turn right on Rue de Marseille if you'd like to go outlet shopping ㉔ ㉕. Turn left on Rue Y. Toudic and then right at the end of the street on Rue Beaurepaire. Visit the Place de la République ㉖ ㉗. Walk back via Rue Dieu and over the bridge. Take Rue Alibert back and turn right on Rue Bichat. Continue to the Goncourt metro station, then turn right onto Avenue Parmentier ㉘. Continue walking, then turn left on Rue Oberkampf for some fun shops ㉙ ㉚. Wander through the bustling Rue Oberkampf, where there are plenty more places to eat ㉛. Turn right on Rue Crespin du Gast to visit the Musée Édith Piaf ㉜ and a rooftop terrace ㉝. End the day at a local watering hole ㉞.

SIGHTS & ATTRACTIONS

9 The largest, most famous cemetery in Paris is the **Cimetière du Père-Lachaise.** This is the final resting place of many famous people, including Oscar Wilde, Marcel Proust, Sidonie-Gabrielle Colette, Édith Piaf, Jim Morrison, and Frédéric Chopin. As you walk through the shaded, chestnut-lined lanes, you'll see graves of all types: mini palaces, crumbling ruins, graves decorated with marble columns, figures of angels, porcelain statues, and much, much more.

8 Boulevard de Ménilmontant (main entrance), 71 Rue des Rondeaux, 16 Rue des Repos, 20th arr., www.pere-lachaise.com, Nov 6-March 15 Mon-Fri 8am-5:30pm, Sat 8:30am-5:30pm, Sun 9am-5:30pm, March 16-Nov 5 Mon-Fri 8am-6pm, Sat 8:30am-6pm, Sun 9am-5:30pm, free, Metro Père Lachaise

12 **Ateliers d'Artistes de Belleville** is an overarching organization for local artists. Their goal is to protect the artistic character of Belleville and to promote its artists. To do so, they organize international exchanges, exhibitions, and courses. More than 250 artists and 20 collectives are connected to the organization from various disciplines. The exhibits are often of photography and paintings and are truly worth the visit.

1 Rue Francis Picabia, 20th arr., www.ateliers-artistes-belleville.fr, see website for opening hours, Metro Couronnes

27 **Place de la République** is one of the liveliest squares in Paris. Located between the hip Canal St Martin and Le Marais, it is a place many people pass through. In the center of the square is the well-known statue of Marianne, the personification of the French Republic. The square is regularly the site of events and protests, and there is almost always something going on here.

Place de la République, 3rd arr., Metro République

32 Édith Piaf was born on December 15, 1915, at number 72 Rue de Belleville. She literally grew up in the streets of Belleville and Ménilmontant. At the **Musée Édith Piaf** you can learn all about her turbulent life through souvenirs,

photos, letters, posters, theater costumes, and more. If you are planning to visit the museum, be sure to make an appointment at least two days beforehand.

5 Rue Crespin du Gast, 11th arr., www.parisinfo.com/musee-monument-paris/71402/musee-edith-piaf, Mon-Wed 1pm-6pm, Thur 10am-noon, closed June & Sept, visit by appointment, free, Metro Ménilmontant

FOOD & DRINK

❶ **La Rotonde Stalingrad** is a great location with something for everyone: a restaurant that also serves brunch, an enormous terrace, and a small bar with music on the weekends. Here they regularly organize a variety of activities, such as flea markets or fashion brunches. See the website for the most up-to-date program.

6-8 Place de la Bataille de Stalingrad, 19th arr., www.larotondestalingrad.com, tel. 01 80483340, Mon 3pm-1am, Tue-Sun noon-1am, €18, Metro Jaurès or Stalingrad

❸ Borrow some chaises lounges and Pétanque balls at the alternative **BarOurcq,** then order your drinks at the bar and head over to the water. Thanks to the DJ music and yummy snacks, such as pigs in a blanket or homemade cake, it is easy to spend an entire evening hanging out here.
68 Quai de la Loire, 19th arr., barourcq.free.fr, tel. 01 42401226, Thu 3pm-midnight, Fri-Sat 3pm-2am, Sun 3pm-10pm, €3, Metro Jaurès or Laumière

❹ The best craft beer in Paris can be found at **Paname Brewing Company,** on the north side of the Quai de la Loire. Find a seat on the waterfront terrace and enjoy a cold beer and casual fare such as pizza, quesadillas, or a burger. The brewery has five standard house beers on offer but also experiments with seasonal beers, which means that every time you visit there's something new to try.
41 Bis Quai de la Loire, 19th arr., www.panamebrewingcompany.com, tel. 01 40364355, daily 11am-2am, special beer €4.50, lunch €11, Metro Laumière or Ourcq

❿ When you're in the mood for a drink, there is no better place to go than **Moncoeur Belleville.** From the terrace, the view out over the rooftops of Paris is downright spectacular, and inside is pleasant too. This is someplace you come more for a drink and the atmosphere than for the food, although the offerings are not at all bad. The venue also organizes regular exhibits, readings, debates, and music shows.
1 Rue des Envierges, 20th arr., www.moncoeurbelleville.com, tel. 01 43663854, Mon-Sun 10am-2am, €16, Sunday brunch €17, Metro Pyrénées

⓭ **Le Baratin** is a great, typical Parisian bistro with a perfect wine menu. Raquel Caréla serves up traditional French fare in her small kitchen. Order a glass of Sagesse de Gramenon with lunch or let them suggest something for you. This is a favorite spot among the locals, so reservations are recommended.
3 Rue Jouye-Rouve, 20th arr., tel. 01 43493970, Tue-Fri noon-2:30pm & 7:30pm-11pm, Sat 7:30pm-11pm, lunch €20, dinner €40, Metro Pyrénées or Belleville

⓮ Finding good vegan and gluten-free food can be a challenge in Paris. But **Zoé Bouillon** offers healthy food that is both delicious and affordable. The friendly staff behind the counter is happy to tell you about their food and set menus. Don't forget to also try the desserts—they are delicious.

66 Rue Rébéval, 19th arr., www.zoebouillon.fr, tel. 01 42020283, Mon-Fri 11:30am-3:30pm & 6:30pm-10:30pm, Sat 11:30am-3:30pm, €12, Metro Pyrénées

⓰ In the mood for a French–Cambodian meal? At **Le Petit Cambodge** you can get lunch or dinner Cambodian style. Slide up to one of the narrow wooden tables and dig in with chopsticks. You can come here any time of the day.

20 Rue Alibert, 10th arr., www.lepetitcambodge.fr, tel. 01 42458088, Mon-Thu & Sun noon-11pm, Fri-Sat noon-11:30pm, €13, Metro République or Goncourt

⓴ **Café A** is in a former monastery and is a place of real calm in the center of the city. This artsy café hosts regular exhibitions, and the tables are decorated with the work of young Parisian artists. Recommended, however, is the garden where you can lean back in a comfy chair and recharge in the sun.

148 Rue du Faubourg Saint-Martin, 10th arr., www.cafea.fr, tel. 09 81298338, Sun & Mon 10am-5pm, Tue-Sat 10am-2am, €15, Metro Gare de l'Est

㉒ Wine bar **Early June** is one of those typical Parisian places where you can easily spend the entire evening. There are delicious wines paired with small sharing plates. Early June hosts different chefs from all over the world, which means the menu is always changing, and there are surprises with each new version.

19 Rue Jean Poulmarch, 10th arr., www.early-june.fr, tel. 01 42854074, Wed-Sun 6pm-1am, €20, Metro Jacques Bonsergent

㉖ At first glance, **Lavomatic** appears to be a normal laundromat. But at this speakeasy, you can do much more than just your laundry. Push a button on one of the machines to open the secret door to a small, intimate cocktail lounge. Don't expect to get a standard mojito here—they serve only one-of-a-kind cocktails made from the best fresh ingredients. Lavomatic is located close to the

PET. NAT ITALIE
CHAMPAGNE   RUPPERT
ROUGES   [ROSÉ] Camarillo Loire
2015 CHINON   SÉBILLE
2013 JURA   P.CLAIRET
2013 SAVOIE   G.BERLIOZ
2014 ITALIE   CALABRE
2011 CÔTES DE DURAS . Jougla
2016 J.NICO - ROUSSILLON
2015 GEVREY - CHAMBERTIN Rateau
2014 MORGON J.Foillard
2013 CHÂTEAU PIQUITA - MAJORQUE

bustling République, making it the perfect starting point for a night on the town.

30 Rue René Boulanger, 10th arr., www.lavomatic.paris, Tues-Wed 6pm-1am, Thur-Sat 6pm-2am, cocktail €9, Metro République

28 The restaurant **Le Chateaubriand** is incredibly popular. And for good reason—the talented young chef, Inaki Aizpitarte, serves up top-quality, innovative dishes in a beautiful, simple, and stylish setting. The wait staff also look sharp, adding that little finishing touch to the restaurant's overall concept. Reservations are an absolute must.

129 Avenue Parmentier, 11th arr., www.lechateaubriand.net, tel. 01 43574595, Tues-Sat 7pm-11pm, set meal €75, Metro Goncourt

31 **Café Charbon** was originally a variety theater where singer Maurice Chevalier made his debut. The grand café, with its dark wood interior and lights that appear to have been hanging for centuries, is always packed on the weekend with young Parisians. Come here at night for a drink, to catch a live show, and maybe even to dance.

109 Rue Oberkampf, 11th arr., www.lecafecharbon.fr, tel. 01 43575513, Sun-Thurs 8am-2am, Fri-Sat 8am-5am, €20, Metro Parmentier

33 **Le Perchoir** has that Parisian *Sex and the City* feel. At this rooftop bar you can lounge with a cocktail in hand while looking out over the city. The clientele is international; residents from all parts of the city come here to meet up. Le Perchoir is not immediately visible from the street. Take the elevator there where the bouncer is standing, and it will bring you up seven stories to the rooftop bar. There is a selection of French bar food to order from, and the restaurant (reservation required) is one floor down.

14 Rue Crespin du Gast, 11th arr., www.leperchoir.fr, tel. 01 48061848, Thur-Sat 6pm-2am, drinks from €13, set meal €48, Metro Ménilmontant or Rue St.-Maur

SHOPPING

6 Anyone looking for unique design items must stop in at **L'Embellie.**
Ceramics, lamps, things for the office, and bags are just a few of the items
from the store's full collection. You can be sure that whatever products you
come across here, you probably won't be able to find anywhere else. The street
is full of pop-up stores that sell local design items. Be sure to stop in and check
out some of them.
14 Rue de la Villette, 19th arr., www.lembellie-design.fr, Tues-Fri 11am-2pm & 4pm-
8pm, Sat 10:30am-7:30pm, Metro Jourdain

19 **Antoine & Lili** are the three brightly colored shops on the Canal Saint-
Martin. One of the stores sells objects from around the world, one sells wom-
en's apparel, and one sells kids' clothes. All three are colorful, multicultural
havens of clothing and kitsch that come in styles ranging from Hindustani to
Mexican. Next to the store's own clothing line, you'll also find all of Antoine and
Lili's favorite brands.
95 Quai de Valmy, 10th arr., www.antoineetlili.com, Mon 1pm-7pm, Tue-Sun 11am-
7pm, Metro République or Goncourt

21 You can't miss the red facade of bookshop **Artazart.** It is one of the best
known in the city and is famous for its selection of design, fashion, signed, and
rare books. The shop also sells fun prints and has an occasional exhibition. It's a
great place to browse!
83 Quai de Valmy, 10th arr., www.artazart.com, daily 10:30am-7:30pm, Metro
Jacques Bonsergent

23 The French brand **LDB** makes stylish and good quality clothing basics. The
brand is sustainable and uses only beautiful fabrics that last a lifetime, such as
cashmere and organic cotton. Their outlet store is here in the 10th arrondissement, but there are more stores throughout Paris that are also worth exploring.
29 Rue des Vinaigriere, 10th arr., www.ldbpariscom, daily 11am-7pm, Metro Jacques
Bonsergent

24 Outlet stores for numerous French brands are tucked away in **Rue de Marseille.** You'll find collections from the previous season and discounted items from stores such as Maje (number 4), Claudie Pierlot (number 6), and Les Petites (number 11). Enjoy browsing through the large selection of dresses, shoes, silk blouses, leather jackets, handbags, and more.

Rue de Marseille, 10th arr., open Mon-Sat 11am-8pm, Sun 1:30pm-7:30pm, Metro Jacques Bonsergent, République, or Goncourt

25 **Centre Commercial** is the perfect shop if you're looking for special French brands, such as Repetto and Isabel Marant. It's also a great spot to find clothes and accessories from up-and-coming designers. All brands sold in the store pay particular attention to quality and to socially and ecologically responsible production, making this the perfect place to pick up beautiful, sustainable items.

2 Rue de Marseille, 10th arr., www.centrecommercial.cc, Sun 2pm-7pm, Mon-Sat 11am-8pm, Metro République

29 The collection of bags, jewelry, and accessories at **Made by Moi** are—as the name suggests—all handmade. Some items are produced in small batches, while others are one of a kind. You'll also find a small selection of clothes and knickknacks here.

86 Rue Oberkampf, 11th arr., www.madebymoi.fr, Tues-Sat 11am-7pm, Metro Parmentier

③⓪ Dresses, skirts, shoes, scarves, hats, kids' clothes, and linens made from traditional African material with a modern Western twist—that is what you'll find at **Africouleur.** All items are also available on the store's website.

108 Rue Saint-Maur, 11th arr., www.africouleur.com, Tues-Wed 10:30am-8pm, Thur-Fri 11am-8pm, Sat 11am-5pm, Metro Rue St-Maur or Parmentier

MORE TO EXPLORE

At the end of a good day, **Bassin de la Villette** is a nice place to walk along the water, stop, sit awhile, have a picnic, or play a game of boules. Groups of friends gather here for picnics and drinks. On both sides of the water are theaters where you can catch a movie. Buy a ticket on the opposite side of the water from where your film is showing, and cross to the other side by boat.

Quai de la Loire, 19th arr., free, Metro Jaurès or Stalingrad

Buttes-Chaumont was once a place of marshy land and chalky soil. In 1864, Napoleon III commissioned the urban architect Haussmann to take control of this no man's land, and in 1867, the **Parc des Buttes-Chaumont** was opened. It is a wonderful landscape of trees, shrubs, stairs, caves, and a big lake. In the lake there is a large rock with a replica of the Temple de Sybille on top, the original of which is in Tivoli. Go up the paths and stairs to the temple, and you'll be rewarded with a surprising view of Sacré-Coeur.

Rue Manin, Rue Botzaris, Avenue Simon-Bolivar, 19th arr., www.paris.fr/lieux/%20 parc-des-buttes-chaumont-1757, daily May-Sep 7am-10pm, Oct-Apr 7am-8pm, free, Metro Buttes-Chaumont or Botzaris

❼ Near the beautiful street Villa de l'Ermitage is the **Studio de l'Ermitage,** with a concert hall, cinema, and theater. Visit the website and see what the program is—it's worth it. Villa l'Ermitage is a bit of countryside in the middle of

Paris. It is nice to walk around, taking photos of the colorfully shuttered houses and admiring the artistic graffiti. Who knows, you might even see an artist busy at work.

8 Rue de l'Ermitage, 20th arr., www.studio-ermitage.com, daily 8:30pm-2am, €8-15, Metro Ménilmontant, Jourdain, or Gambetta

🟤 The Sunday jazz brunch at **La Bellevilloise** always draws a crowd. Enjoy a buffet of sweet and savory French fare under the olive trees in the Halle aux Oliviers and be sure to check out the program beforehand so you're up to date on what's going on in this cultural center. Exhibits, dance, concerts, clubs—anything is possible. The clientele at La Bellevilloise is hip and alternative. Next door, La Maroquinerie (at 23 Rue Boyer) is a similar sort of venue, with cultural events and a restaurant where you can head for an enjoyable evening.

19-21 Rue Boyer, 19th arr., www.labellevilloise.com, Thur-Sat 6:30pm-1am, Sun 11:30am-2pm, entrance €10-20, jazz brunch €29, Metro Ménilmontant, Jourdain, or Gambetta

🔟 Built in 1988 against a steep hill, **Parc de Belleville** is the highest park in Paris. Albeit small, the park is not to be missed. Go there, even if only to see the phenomenal view of the city. Walk down the beautiful paths—up and down stairs, past springs that once supplied the city's water, and along waterfalls that feed into lakes below.

Rue Piat, Rue des Couronnes, Rue Julien-Lacroix, 20th arr., www.paris.fr/equipements/parc-de-belleville-1777, daily, free, Metro Pyrénées or Couronnes

🟤 **Place Sainte-Marthe** is one of Paris's best hidden gems. Savor the calm in one of two bistros. There are often musicians on the square, and sometimes there are small theater performances.

Place Sainte-Marthe, 10th arr., Metro Colonel Fabien or Belleville

🟤 Built between 1821 and 1825, **Canal Saint-Martin** is about 2.5 miles (4 km) long. A system of locks regulates the water levels, which differ for 82 feet (25 m) from one end of the canal to the other. The beautiful cast-iron bridges appear in movies such as *Amélie* when the main character skips stones over the water.

The up-and-coming neighborhood around the canal is full of nice cafés and unique clothing stores.

Le Canal Saint-Martin, 10th arr., Metro République or Goncourt

⑱ Le Comptoir Général is hard to describe. It is an alternative hub of the kind you might come across in Berlin or Barcelona but not often in Paris. This cultural center was built in an old 6,500 square foot (600 sq m) stable and is decorated in French African colonial style. The shabby-chic décor gives it a mysterious atmosphere. There are many hidden nooks where you might come across a curio cabinet, or a glass case filled with exotic plants. Order a fresh ginger juice at the bar or eat fried banana in the restaurant, which is more of a dining hall where you're never at a table by yourself. This is a great spot for an aperitif, brunch, a cultural reading, or a film.

84 Quai de Jemmapes, 10th arr., www.lecomptoirgeneral.com, Tue-Wed 6pm-1am, Thur-Fri 6pm-2am, Sat 11am-2am, Sun 11am-1am, voluntary donation, Metro République or Goncourt

㉞ Gossima Ping Pong Bar is Paris's first Ping-Pong bar, where you not only can get something to drink but you can also play table tennis. Come with friends to this spacious bar full of Ping-Pong tables for a night of fun and games—it's a good alternative to a pool hall. On Friday evenings, the venue occasionally organizes Ping-Pong disco night. The crowd here is primarily twenty- and thirty-somethings.

4 Rue Victor Gelez, 11th arr., www.gossima.fr, Mon 4pm-midnight, Tue-Sat 4pm-2am, free, Ping-Pong table rental €6, Metro Ménilmontant or Rue St.-Maur

WITH MORE TIME

The walks in this book will take you to most of the city's main highlights. Of course, there are still several places worth visiting and things worth seeing that are not included. We have listed some of them below. Note that not all these places are easily accessible on foot from central Paris, but they can all be reached with public transportation.

(A) In 2014, a dilapidated station along the line known as La Petite Ceinture in the 18th arrondissement in northern Paris was spruced up. Now you can head to **La REcyclerie** for brunch (Saturday and Sunday), lunch, dinner, or a drink. It's a delightful place to sit on a warm summer's night—out in the fresh air at one of the long tables amid the colorful lights. Events such as flea markets and workshops are regularly held here. Combine La Recyclerie with a trip to the flea market Marché aux Puces de Saint-Ouen, which is not far away.

83 Boulevard Ornano, 18th arr., www.larecyclerie.com, daily noon-10pm, lunch €14, brunch €23, Metro Porte de Clignancourt

(B) At the marchés aux puces (flea markets) you can come across some good finds, but don't count on them always being inexpensive. **Marché aux Puces de Saint-Ouen** is Paris's largest antique and flea market—it is an entire village of antique shops. The flea market is often used as a backdrop in movies, such as *Midnight in Paris*. There are also several nice cafés here for lunch, such as the guinguette Chez Louisette (136 Avenue Michelet), where real French chansons are sung live.

Avenue de la Porte de Clignancourt, 18th arr., www.marcheauxpuces-saintouen.com, Mon 11am-5pm, Fri 8am-noon, Sat-Sun 10am-6pm, Metro Porte de Clignancourt

(C) In the middle of the Bois de Boulogne you'll find the museum **Fondation Louis Vuitton,** which opened in 2015. The futuristic building, which was designed by Frank Gehry, makes it worth a visit. Inside, you'll find a permanent collection as well as temporary exhibits of modern and contemporary art. Occasionally there are classical concerts. Come to the restaurant Le Frank for

an outstanding lunch and, on Wednesday and Thursday evenings, for dinner (reservations required).

8 Avenue du Mahatma Gandhi, 16th arr., www.fondationlouisvuitton.fr, Mon-Thur 10am-8pm, Fri 10am-11pm, Sat-Sun 9am-9pm, entrance €16, Metro les Sablons (15-minute walk) or shuttle bus from Place Charles de Gaulle (corner of Avenue de Friedland)

Ⓓ **La Cinémathèque Française** is located in the former Centre Culturel Américain, a building designed by architect Frank Gehry. The archive contains some 40,000 films and an enormous collection of documents, manuscripts, and posters. In addition to the permanent exhibit about the history of film, there are also exhibits with unique film showings and talks.

51 Rue de Bercy, 12th arr., www.cinematheque.fr, Mon & Wed-Fri noon-7pm, Sat-Sun 11am-8pm, museum €10, film €7, Metro Bercy

Ⓔ From 1859 to 1969 train tracks ran across **Le Viaduc des Arts.** In 1996 it was transformed into a promenade plantée: a park that is about 3 miles (5 km) long. Take the stairs at the beginning of the street and walk over the 64 red brick arches. In the archways, you'll find artist studios and shops.

1-129 Avenue Daumesnil, 12th arr., www.leviaducdesarts.com, Mon-Sat 9am-6pm, free, Metro Bastille

(F) **Parc de la Villette** focuses on science and art. The futuristic municipal park has been around since 1986 and has, among other things, a playground, a concert hall, an IMAX theater (La Géode) and a variety of museums. Visit, for example, the Cité des Sciences et de l'Industrie (science museum) and the Cité de la Musique/Philharmonie de Paris (music museum). The park is full of activity, such as movies in the open-air theater in July and August. Check out the website for the latest program. You can easily spend the entire day here.

211 Avenue Jean Jaurès, 19th arr., www.villette.com, daily, free to park, museums €7-€16, Metro Porte de Pantin / Porte de la Villette

(G) **La Tour Montparnasse** is a typical 20th-century monument—686 feet (209m) tall, with the fastest elevator in Europe, which brings you to the top floor in just 38 seconds. On the 56th floor there is a fantastic panoramic view of Paris and, when the weather is clear, of the entire Île de France. You can see as far as 25 miles (40 km) away. Daring visitors can go to the open terrace two stories above.

33 Avenue du Maine, 15th arr., www.tourmontparnasse56.com, daily 11am-10:30pm, €17, Metro Montparnasse-Bienvenüe

(H) Face the lines and journey into Paris's underworld. Descend 91 steps below ground into the world of the dead and see bones from old burial grounds. There are countless myths about the **Catacombes.** It is cold here, so bring an extra layer.

1 Avenue du Colonel Henri Rol-Tanguy, 14th arr., www.catacombes.paris.fr, Tue-Sun 9:45am-8:30pm, €29, Metro Denfert-Rochereau

(I) The **Musée Jacquemart-André** was originally the private residence of enthusiastic art collectors. There is a very diverse art collection on display from the 18th century and from the Italian Renaissance. The luxurious tearoom is a nice spot for Sunday brunch.

158 Boulevard Haussmann, 8th arr., www.musee-jacquemart-andre.com, Mon 10am-8:30pm, Tue-Sun 10am-6pm, €17, Metro St.-Philippe du Roule / Miromesnil / St.-Augustin

(J) The **Marché Aligre** is a lively vegetable market that makes for a busy street scene on Saturdays and Sundays. Locals meet here to chat about the past week over wine at Le Baron Rouge (1 Rue Théophile Roussel), one of the many cafés at the market.

Place d'Aligre, 12th arr., indoor market Tue-Fri 9am-1pm & 4pm-5:30pm, Sat 9am-1pm & 3:30pm-7:30pm, Sun 9am-1:30pm, outdoor market Tue-Fri 7:30am-1:30pm, Sat-Sun 7:30am-2:30pm, Metro Ledru-Rollin

(K) **Musée Marmottan Monet** is particularly known for its collection of works by Impressionist painter Claude Monet. Also in this beautiful 19th-century building you'll find artwork from the Renaissance and the First Empire. When you're on this side of Paris, reserve a table at the restaurant La Gare (19 Chaussée de la Muette). In this former train station, you can enjoy a delicious meal in a unique environment.

2 Rue Louis Boilly, 16th arr., www.marmottan.fr, Tue-Wed & Sat-Sun 10am-6pm, Thur 10am-9pm, €12, Metro la Muette

(L) At the metro station Passy, right around the corner, is a sort of underground wine cellar: **Musée du Vin.** Visit the interesting and beautiful exhibit about how wine is made, the techniques used in the past and the present, and all the various objects involved in wine making. It is not big—you'll have seen it all in less than an hour. If you know you'll have more time than that, make reservations beforehand for a wine tasting or enjoy lunch in the restaurant. It goes without saying that a nice wine is paired with every course.

5 Square Charles Dickens, 16th arr., www.museeduvinparis.com, museum open Tue-Sat 10am-6pm, restaurant open Tue-Sat noon-3pm, museum €12.50, Metro Passy

(M) Within a half hour of Paris you can be in the nice town of Versailles, known for the enormous **Château de Versailles.** This 1631 palace has a rich history. France was ruled from here from 1681 to 1789. The imposing complex, with its enormous gardens, halls, outbuildings, and status symbols, leave a special impression. You could easily spend several days here. In the summer there are firework shows at night. Tip: buy your ticket online beforehand.

Place d'Armes, Versailles, www.chateauversailles.fr, castle April-Oct Tues-Sun 9am-6:30pm, park daily 8am-8:30pm, Nov-March Tues-Sun 9am-5:30pm, park daily 8am-6pm, free for the park, castle €18 (free first Sunday of month), take the RER C train from Saint-Michel or Champ de Mars to Versailles Rive Gauche

INDEX

MOON
PARIS WALKS
THIRD EDITION

AVALON TRAVEL
Hachette Book Group
1700 Fourth Street
Berkeley, CA 94710, USA
www.moon.com

ISBN 979-8-88647-022-2
Concept & Original Publication
"time to momo Paris"
© 2024 by mo'media.
All rights reserved.

time to momo

(m)

MO'MEDIA

Text & Walks
Roosje Nieman

Translation
Cindi Heller

Photography
Vincent van den Hoogen,
Dani van Oeffelen,
Duncan de Fey

Design
Studio 100%, Oranje Vormgevers

Project Editor
Sanne van der Kolk

AVALON TRAVEL

Project Editor
Lori Hobkirk

Typesetting
Timm Bryson

Cartography
Brian Shotwell, Erin Greb,
Kat Bennett, Mike Morgenfeld

Copy Editor
Lori Hobkirk

Proofreader
Sandy Chapman

Cover Design
Faceout Studio, Jeff Miller

Printed in China by RR Donnelley
First US printing, February 2024

CREATE AN EPIC TRAVEL BUCKET LIST

WANDERLUST
Road Trips
40 BEAUTIFUL DRIVES AROUND THE WORLD

EXPLORE CITY NEIGHBORHOOD WALKS